CW01654575

EARL'S COURT AND BROMPTON PAST

Dedicated to the memory of

BARBARA DENNY (*d*.1998)

author of *Fulham Past, Notting Hill & Holland Park Past, Hammersmith & Shepherds Bush Past, Chelsea Past* and *Kensington Past*
She is much missed

The Illustrations

We would like to thank the Royal Borough of Kensington and Chelsea for permission to reproduce most of the illustrations in this book. We would also like to thank the London Borough of Hackney Archives Department and the National Film Archive for the use of pictures *166* and *126* respectively. The author, Richard Tames supplied *94, 97, 100, 127, 146, 147, 148, 149, 150* and *151*, and the publishers, , Historical Publications, supplied *20, 72, 103, 105, 107, 118, 130, 140, 141*.

First published 2000
by Historical Publications Ltd
32 Ellington Street, London N7 8PL
(Tel: 020-7607 1628)

© **Richard Tames 2000**
The moral right of the author has been asserted
All rights reserved; unauthorised duplication contravenes applicable laws

ISBN 0 948667 63 X
British Library Cataloguing-in-Publication Data
A catalogue record for this book is available from the British Library

Typeset in Palatino by Historical Publications Ltd
Reproduction by G & J Graphics, London EC2
Printed in Zaragoza, Spain by Edelvives.

EARLS COURT AND BROMPTON PAST

Richard Tames

with illustrations chosen by
Carolyn Starren

HISTORICAL PUBLICATIONS

Introduction

From fertile farmland to fashionable faubourg in a single lifetime – such was the transformation of the area covered by this book, at least as far as it might be summarised in a single sentence. Fashionableness, it must be conceded, tended to fade away the further west one went. As late as the 1820s the locality was still an Elysium of nurseries and market gardens, punctuated by the occasional villa, tavern or short residential terrace, bisected by a single turnpike road and traversed by dusty, straggling lanes. By the 1880s it was covered with well-paved streets of Italianate, Gothic and 'Queen Anne' houses, interspersed with communal gardens, churches and shopping parades and integrated into the larger metropolis by busy highways and railway lines. The territory now covered by the Royal Borough of Kensington and Chelsea – of which the area covered by this book forms only a part, but perhaps one of the most densely populated – had a population of just over eight thousand at the time of the first census in 1801; about the same as a small market town. By 1901 the figure was over twenty times as great, putting it on a par with a substantial provincial city like Cardiff.

Apart from the general forces underlying the expansion of the metropolis as a whole, most notably the growth of London as a global trading and financial centre, two specific factors underpinned the development of the Earl's Court and Brompton area – the 1851 Exhibition and the Underground.

The Great Exhibition of the Arts and Industry of All Nations, held in Hyde Park in 1851, was the first 'world fair'. To attribute its conception and astonishing success solely to Albert, Queen Victoria's Prince Consort, would be to undervalue the contribution of the brilliant team of administrators, engineers and entrepreneurs gathered around him to realize his vision. But his remains the presiding spirit behind 'South Ken', a term which originally defined not merely a specific location but a view of culture, industry, science and their relationship to one another. The Great Exhibition made a profit of £186,000, part of which was used to buy some ninety acres of land stretching southwards from Kensington Gore. This was to become 'Albertopolis', a complex of museums, colleges and learned institutions intended to perpetuate the humanistic

1. The Old Brompton Road in 1822 – piecemeal development and open views.

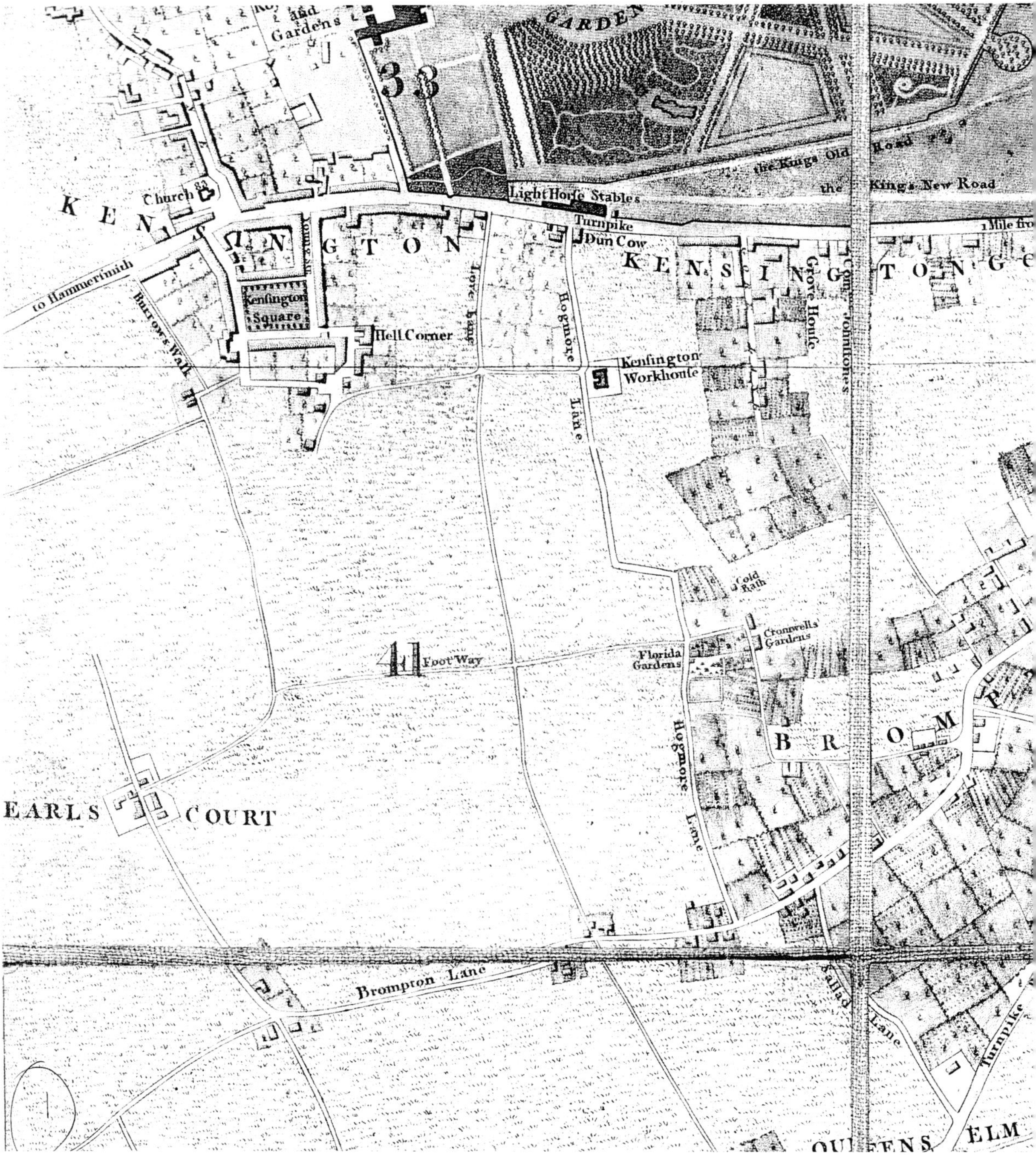

2. Cary's map of the area in 1787 with Kensington Gardens to the north. Earl's Court is entirely rural and Brompton is mostly market gardens. Florida Gardens and Cromwell Gardens are in the centre, and the beginnings of Michael's Place is to the east off Brompton Row. Across the road is a wax candle factory and top right of the map is a floor tile manufacturer.

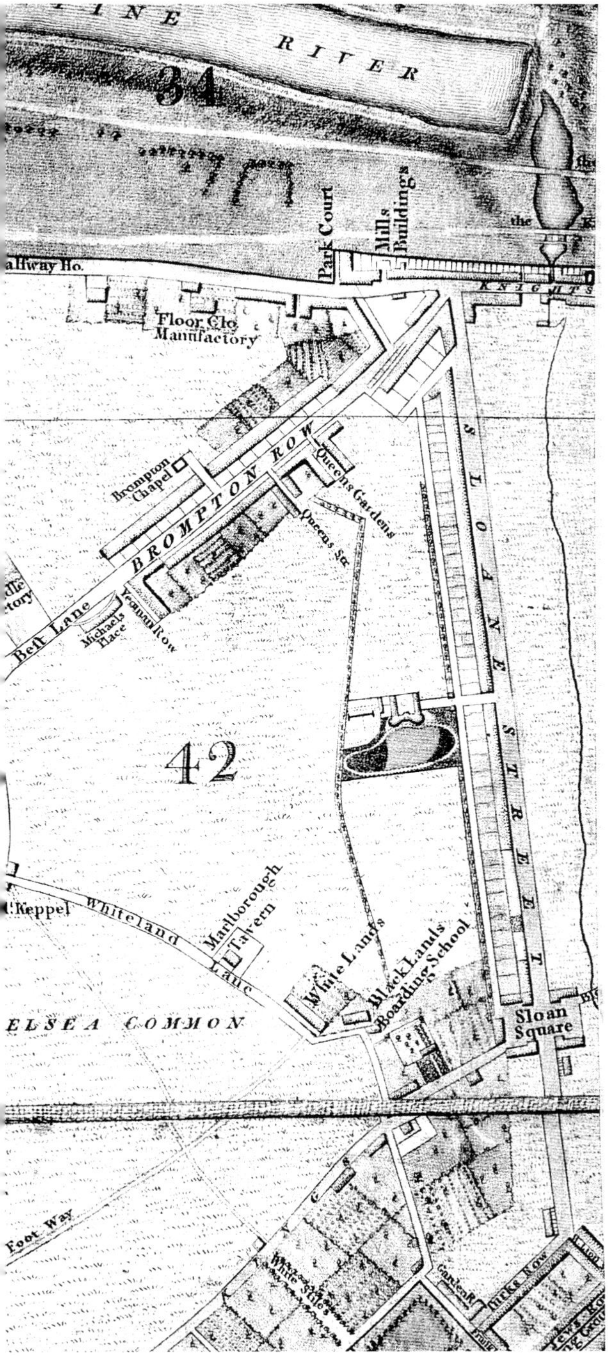

3. *The Westbourne river at 'Knight's Bridge'. The river rose in Hampstead and was used to form the Serpentine in Hyde Park, from where it went just to the east of Sloane Street to the Thames. It is now carried over the tracks at Sloane Square station in an iron tube.*

interplay of the arts and sciences and their practical application to the world of work which the Exhibition itself had represented.

Although the development of streets, squares and crescents on the Smith's Charity and Alexander estates was well advanced even before the Great Exhibition, it was acknowledged at the time of its successor, the all-but-forgotten International Exhibition of 1862, that its location was still difficult of access. This deficiency was remedied by 1870 with the opening of South Kensington, Gloucester Road and Earl's Court stations, leading to a final burst of building activity, completed by the construction of major mansion blocks in the 1890s.

While most building development was undertaken on behalf of corporate or family estates, the financial risks were largely borne by speculative builders. Sir Charles Freake (*see p. 36*), who began life as a jobbing carpenter, not only made a fortune but achieved personal eminence

THE + RESIDENCE

is of modern construction (having been erected about twelve years ago under skilled supervision),

of artistic elevation,

and is planned in a particularly convenient manner, every detail for the comfort of the occupants having had special consideration and attention.

In addition to the

PRINCIPAL AND SECONDARY STAIRCASES

there is a

HYDRAULIC PASSENGER LIFT

to all the floors up to the fourth storey.

FINE BILLIARD ROOM.

Dinner Lift. Electric Light. Speaking Tubes.

Many thousands of pounds have been expended upon the property in improvements and embellishments, but this outlay will now be sacrificed to the benefit of a purchaser, as the Vendor has determined to sell regardless of cost.

4. An advertisement of 1906 for a house at 192 Queen's Gate, a road which formed one of the most prestigious developments in the area. The hydraulic passenger lift was probably powered by the London Hydraulic Co. whose network of pipes spread all over central London.

through doing so. Many were less financially adept and bankruptcy was a common fate. The tangled affairs of the second Lord Kensington showed that even landowners could come badly adrift. Builders were much more at risk. James Bonnin senior (?1782-1850), who built Brompton Square, Alexander Place, Trevor Square and much else besides, crashed in 1846. His son, James junior, met the same fate in 1848. James senior persuaded the Kensington Board of Guardians to subsidise his emigration to Adelaide, only to die there of 'natural decay' within a fortnight of making landfall. His son, however, recovered his fortunes and returned to the fray. The firm of Corbett and McClymont, active on both the Edwardes and Gunter estates, went down for a spectacular £1,500,000 in 1878.

What was achieved, however, was widely commended. The German cultural attaché Hermann Muthesius, who had been sent to Britain by the Prussian government with a specific brief to study domestic housing, was lavish in his praise of Evelyn Gardens: "In this system of unbuilt-up garden squares the layout of London's residential quarter may almost be described as exemplary."

The superiority of the built environment was paralleled by the distinction of its inhabitants. A theatrical 'set' congregated in Brompton Square from its very beginnings and a similar presence has been maintained in the locality ever since, through the days of W.S. Gilbert, Ellen Terry and Beerbohm Tree to Gielgud, Rattigan and Emlyn Williams and, more recently, Dirk Bogarde, Anthony Hopkins and Andrew Lloyd Webber. Artists and architects, scientists and sculptors, intellectuals and imperialists were to be found in similar abundance, surrounded by a general population of professionals and *rentiers*. The census of 1871 showed, for example, that there were in Queen's Gate and the nine Streets, Places or Terraces leading into it, some 288 households.

5. *Cottages at Earl's Court c.1836. Watercolour, artist unknown.*

Few residents of this complex would have been regarded as being of national eminence, apart perhaps from the painter Millais and the then current Home Secretary, but there were dozens who might be rated as their social equals or even betters – the widows of Prime Minister Lord Derby and of Radical Free Trader Richard Cobden, a future Lord Chancellor, the son of tycoon railway contractor Thomas Brassey, a grandson of William IV and his actress mistress Mrs Jordan and, even more exotic, the son and the grandson of Napoleon's marshal and King of Naples, Joachim Murat. Along with the Earl of Durham and the Duke of St Albans the residents included twenty-eight other persons of title, plus nineteen MPs, four simply self-styled as 'gentleman' and the clearly self-impressed Sir Coutts Lindsay "artist and dilettante, also of Balcarres, Fife". Over ten per cent of households were occupied by military and naval personnel, serving or retired, and even more by judges, barristers or solicitors. There were also eleven JPs. Other professions were, by contrast, but thinly represented – two engineers, three clergymen, four medical men and five bankers, plus ten civil servants and colonial officials. Twenty-eight households, another ten per cent, were headed by merchants. Only four householders were listed as being primarily partners or directors of major businesses but there were also those who classified themselves as proprietors of houses, steamships, racehorses, a slate quarry, the Broadwood piano business and the Perkins, Whitbread, Courage and Charrington breweries, plus the owner of the *Manchester Guardian*. In addition five heads of household had been directly concerned with either building the area or financing its construction. Over a third of all households were headed by *rentiers* or the retired. Almost one household in six was, at the time of the census, occupied by a caretaker, housekeeper or other servant on behalf of an absent owner who was either working or travelling abroad or, it still being only April, more likely resident in the country, the London 'Season' not starting for some weeks yet.

It comes almost as a relief to know that a neighbourhood of such conspicuous respectabil-

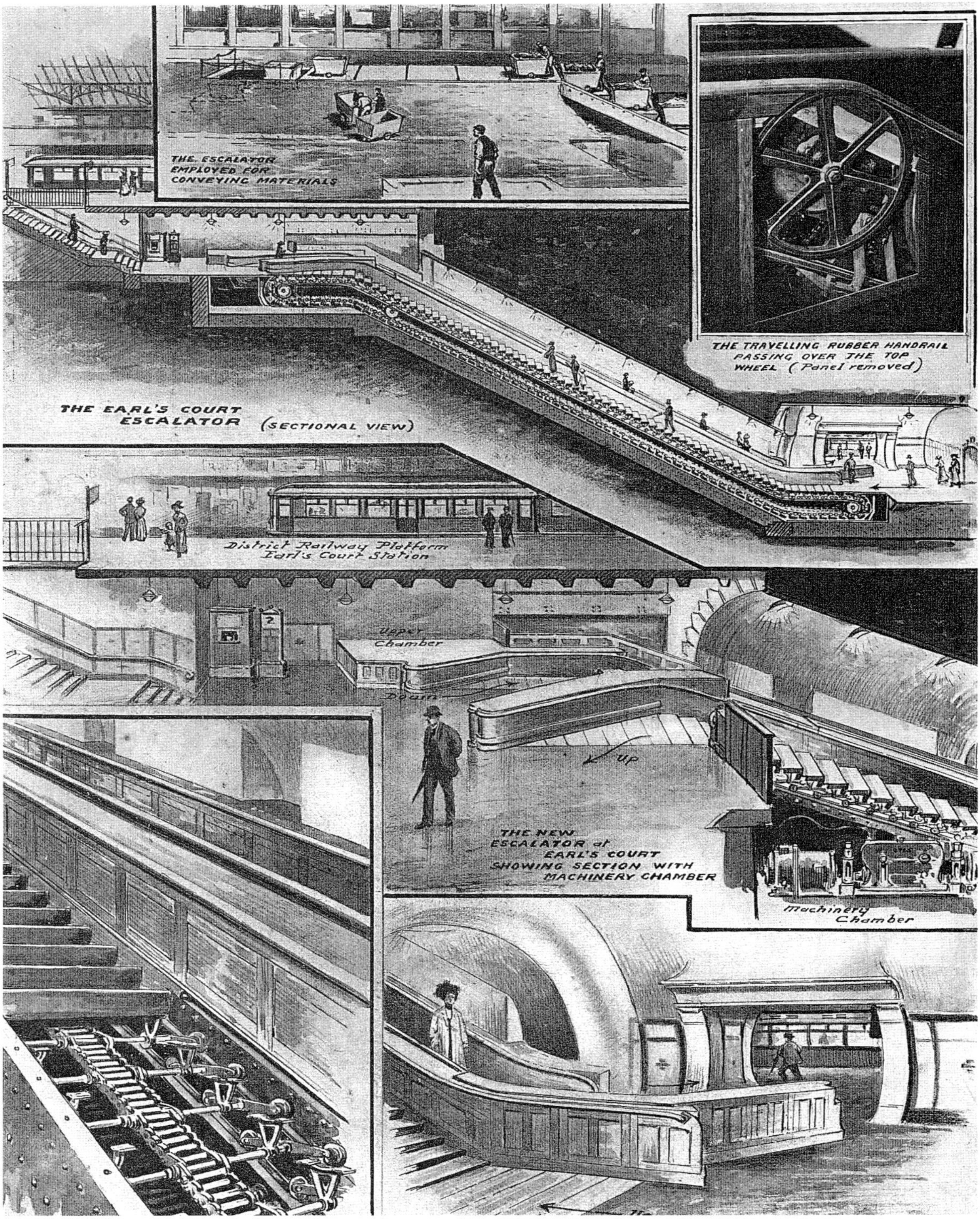

6. An intricate drawing by W.B. Robinson of the new escalator at Earl's Court station, in the Illustrated London News 14 Oct 1911.

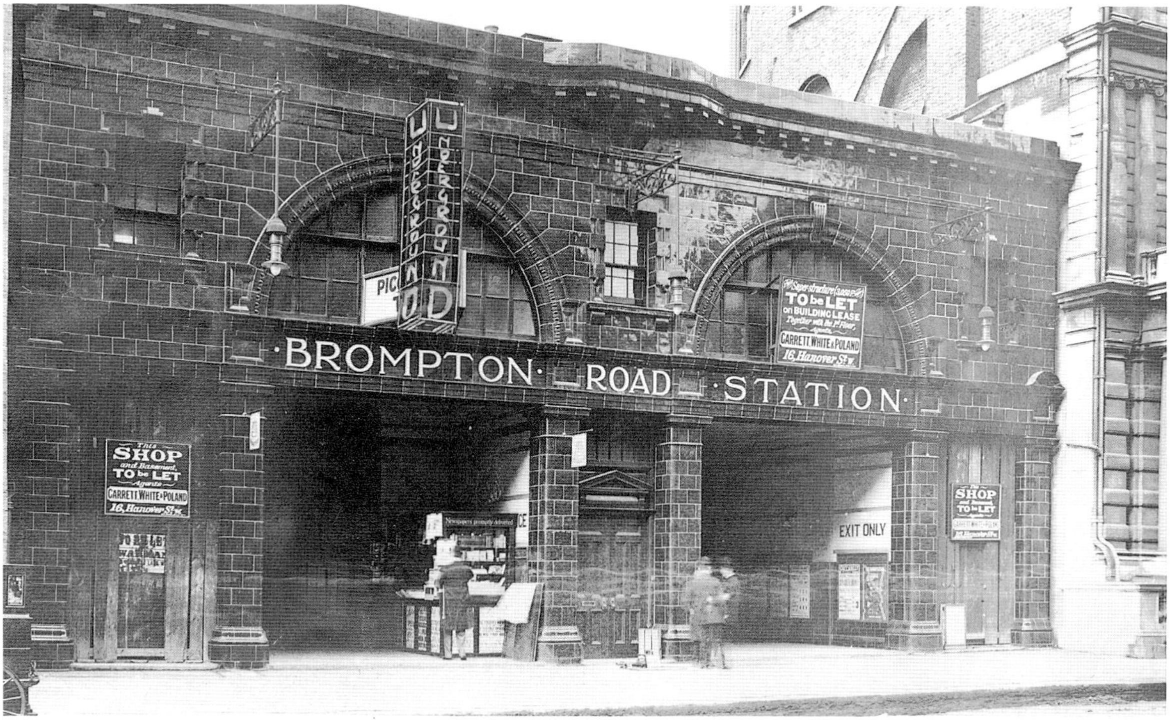

7. Brompton Road, a station between Knightsbridge and South Kensington, was opened on what became the Piccadilly Line in December 1906. Planned to take advantage of the nearby museum attractions, it was located at 206 Brompton Road between Brompton Oratory and Brompton Square, but due to lack of customers it was closed in 1934. It was decorated by Leslie Green in his landmark ox-blood red tiles.

ity has also been home to many distinguished, if usually discreet, members of more Bohemian circles, from the original of Wilde's Dorian Gray to the outrageous painter Francis Bacon. A darker side has also existed. In premises opposite Gloucester Road station, where frivolous Florida Gardens once briefly flourished, Haigh, the 'Acid Bath Murderer', killed and dissolved at least three of his victims. Kim Philby was possibly recruited to the KGB at 3 Rosary Gardens, a building owned by the Soviet consulate. In the 1930s MI5 was headquartered in cramped premises on the Cromwell Road.

As a residential area with a high proportion of middle-aged or elderly or, if young, often temporary, inhabitants Earl's Court and Brompton has probably had a local birth-rate rather below the metropolitan average. The area has, however, been the birthplace and childhood home of talents as varied as children's writer Beatrix Potter, archaeologist Howard Carter and architect Sir Edwin Lutyens. In a slightly different sense, although it can claim no great industrial or technological heritage, it has also been the birthplace of the Hansom cab, the escalator and the 'Rawlplug'. Rawlplugs were developed out of Rawlings Bros. garage in Ashburn Mews, where George Rawlings invented the fibre plug for fixing electrical wall fittings at the British Museum. Re-established in 1921 as the Rawlplug Co. Ltd at 87A and 89 Cromwell Road, by 1939 it had become a global business.

Apart from Albertopolis, the Earl's Court-Brompton nexus is also home to more than a dozen places of worship, most notably the Brompton Oratory, and in Brompton Cemetery, to a major necropolis. To many outsiders, however, the area has become synonymous with pleasures of this world, rather than the hope or consolations of the next – viz. Harrod's, Harvey Nichols and the boutiques of Beauchamp Place, smart hotels and even smarter restaurants. A hinterland of 'Sloane Rangers', Brompton at least is peppered with royal warrant-holders, from corsetières Rigby & Peller to the Casson Conder architectural partnership and Calman Links, the royal furrier. The late Diana, Princess of Wales and Sophie Rhys-Jones, Countess of Wessex, both

8. Coleherne Court marks the boundary between Brompton and Earl's Court. The flats included a servant's bedroom.

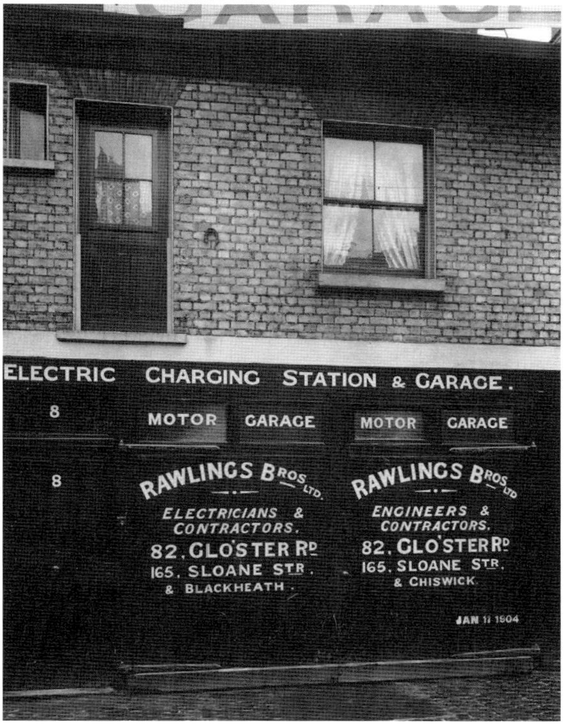

9. *The famous invention, the Rawlplug, began here with Rawlings Bros in a garage in Ashburn Mews.*

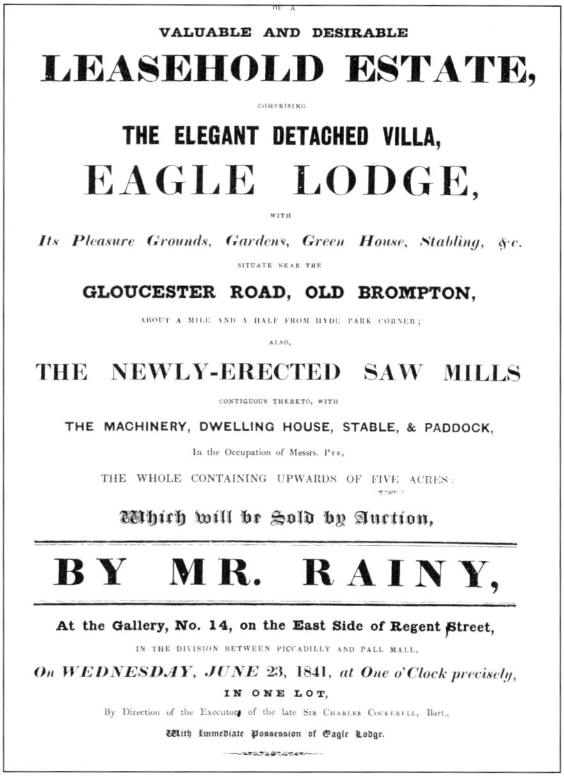

OF A

VALUABLE AND DESIRABLE

LEASEHOLD ESTATE,

COMPRISING

THE ELEGANT DETACHED VILLA,

EAGLE LODGE,

WITH

Its Pleasure Grounds, Gardens, Green House, Stabling, &c.

SITUATE NEAR THE

GLOUCESTER ROAD, OLD BROMPTON,

ABOUT A MILE AND A HALF FROM HYDE PARK CORNER;

ALSO,

THE NEWLY-ERECTED SAW MILLS

CONTIGUOUS THERETO, WITH

THE MACHINERY, DWELLING HOUSE, STABLE, & PADDOCK,

In the Occupation of Messrs. PYE,

THE WHOLE CONTAINING UPWARDS OF FIVE ACRES:

Which will be Sold by Auction,

BY MR. RAINY,

At the Gallery, No. 14, on the East Side of Regent Street,

IN THE DIVISION BETWEEN PICCADILLY AND PALL MALL,

On WEDNESDAY, JUNE 23, 1841, at One o'Clock precisely,

IN ONE LOT,

By Direction of the Executors of the late SIR CHARLES COCKERELL, Bart.,

With Immediate Possession of Eagle Lodge.

10. *Eagle Lodge in Gloucester Road was put up for sale in 1841, together with some newly-erected saw mills. Its site is now covered by Roland Gardens.*

had apartments in Coleherne Court when they were single girls about town.

Standing as it were in the boundary zone of Earl's Court and Brompton the towering mansion block of Coleherne Court offers its inhabitants the choice of wandering eastwards into elegance or westwards into what immediately after World War Two was known from its refugee population as 'the Polish corridor' but swiftly became 'Kangaroo Valley' and is now so diversely cosmopolitan as to defy stereotyping. Author Jonathan Raban noted in the early 1970s the proliferation of local graffiti in non-European scripts and characterised Earl's Court as an unwitting seismograph of global politics and population movement. The backwash of this phenomenon has not always been positive. A 1995 bid for a multi-million pound grant from the then Conservative Government's Single Regeneration Budget Challenge Fund, entitled *Earl's Court at the Crossroads,* pointed out that one in seven of the local residents was unemployed and that over sixty commercial buildings in the locality were seriously dilapidated. Earl's Court Ward, with a 1991 population of 9,377, was one of the most densely populated areas in the entire country. In demographic terms it was also one of the most mobile, with an annual turnover of 30%. Almost half of all local inhabitants had been born outside the United Kingdom. With 4,400 bedspaces in sixty local hotels and ten hostels and 18,000,000 persons passing through Earl's Court station annually the area could certainly claim 'gateway' status as far as the metropolis was concerned. Yet, although this volatile population could scarcely claim to constitute a community, embedded within it there certainly was one, comprised of the inhabitants of the intimate, interlocking streets of 'Earl's Court Village', whose residents were overwhelmingly long-term occupants, determined to protect their locality from what the bid document characterised as the triple threat of "street crime, a dilapidated street environment and sleaze".

Beneath the preoccupations and problems of the present lie lost layers of human history which a book of this brevity can only in part recall.

11. Earl's Court Road c.1960.

12. Brompton Chapel, now part of the buildings used by Bonham's, the auctioneers.

Coleherne Court, itself just short of a century old at the turning of the millennium, was, in the eighteenth century, the site of Coleherne House, rural retreat of poet-physician Sir Richard Blackmore. In 1815 Hereford House was built in its garden. This became the home of dramatist Charles Dance and theatrical managers Benjamin Lumley and Dion Boucicault. Roland Gardens, a development of 1870-92, covers the site of Eagle Lodge where, between 1825 and 1835 its occupant, Samuel Brown, developed the first practical gas engine – a technical achievement which defeated the combined labours of the Brunels, father and son. In 1836 the occupancy of Eagle Lodge passed to Alfred Bunn, manager of Drury Lane Theatre, but he went bankrupt in 1840 (*see p. 97*). From 1855 to 1858 Eagle Lodge was the home of Tom Taylor, editor of *Punch*. As Taylor moved in, a sawmill, established in the grounds of the Lodge in 1837, closed down, to be replaced by a racquet court and a bowling green, which lasted only until 1860. From 1876 to 1881 the area now covered by Nos. 40-46 and 37-49 was a roller-skating rink.

Far more spectacular features have also completely vanished from the scene. The extensive grounds of the Royal Horticultural Society once stretched from where the Albert Hall now stands

13. *Queen's Gate Mansions at the turn of the 20th century, an attempt at contemporary Parisian grandeur.*

AU COIN DU FEU RESTAURANT
Phillimore Gardens
Kensington High Street
WES 5580
CUISINE FRANÇAISE, AMBIANCE INTIME, BON VIN, BON APETIT
Open daily till midnight—including Sundays

FOR CHAUFFEUR-DRIVEN LIMOUSINES & SALOONS
SATCHELLS CAR HIRE
1 PEMBROKE MEWS, W.8
TEL: WEStern 7170/6270

The
EARLS COURTIER

7th September 1962 — Published Fortnightly - No. SIX — PRICE 3d.

THE NEWSPAPER FOR OVERSEAS VISITORS

COMMONWEALTH AT OLYMPIA'S FOOD FAIR

SOUTH AFRICA, Australia and New Zealand were well represented at Britain's 1962 Food Fair which was opened at Olympia this week by the President of the Board of Trade, the Right Hon. Frederick Erroll.

An outstanding feature of the South African stand (No. 346 on the first floor of the Empire Hall) is the display of "Cape Fruit" ranging from grapes to pears. Also represented is South Africa's wine growing industry, established over 300 years ago, producing sherries, excellent white and red dry wines, brandies and the popular liqueur Van der Hum.

Its cheese and butter are being specialised in at the New Zealand stand and fourteen New Zealand girls will present every purchaser of cheese or butter with a 16 page recipe book.

Australia is offering the chance of boomerang visits at Britain's Food Fair, Olympia. Australian girls will give every hundredth customer a boomerang and a complimentary ticket so that they or their friends can make a return visit to the Fair.

The stand is striking, compact and hard-selling with the theme "Look for the word Australia".

A feature of the stand is the Australian wines, 100 bottles of different labels displayed on a back-lighted wall.

The girls staffing the Australian stand come from many parts of Australia.

The promoters of the Fair, which will remain open until September 12th, have set aside four days for special attractions, in addition to the ordinary events and demonstrations.

The first is "Children's Day" on September 1st when all activities will be with an eye to the young generation. On that day there will be cooking contests and demonstrations aimed at young cooks.

"International Food Day" will be on September 6th when home exhibitors will show the international flavour of their products, and overseas stands will stage special promotions. Two days later couples married during the preceding days of the Fair are being invited by the organisers as their guests, and the first fifty couples to sign in will receive a fully stocked hamper. Individual exhibitors are also arranging gifts. These range from bottles of champagne to food parcels with the house-warming of the newly-weds in view.

September 10th will be "Sportsman's Day" and products promoting health and energy will be linked up with the theme.

Prices of admission to the Fair which can be reached by train in five minutes from Earls Court is 3/- for adults and 1/6d. for children (1/- on Sept. 1st).

A MODERN UTOPIA

Britishers Seek New Life

A GROUP of idealists in West London are in the process of putting into operation an idea of one of their number, Mr. Bernard Stanbury. It is formation of an ideal community on an island in the Great Barrier Reef off Australia. A nucleus of the community has already been recruited and has headquarters at Shepherd's Bush. The island has not yet been found. When it is its inhabitants will have no internal currency, no set religion and there will be no competitiveness. Altogether nearly 5,000 applications to join the community have been received. But Mr. Stanbury is selective, and the majority of those anxious to "get away from it all" have been turned down. Only those prepared to pull their weight are required. Slackers and those with "back to nature" aspirations are not wanted. Neither are bomb dodgers.

NEW SHORT STORY COMPETITION

CAN you write a story on your travel experiences? Here is the chance you have been waiting for.

The *Earls Courtier* is offering a First Prize of 5 guineas to the writer of the BEST travel story of not more than 1,200 words received before Oct. 31st, 1962. The winning story will be published in the mid-month edition of this newspaper in November, and the writer of any other story subsequently printed will receive payment of 2 guineas.

Stories will automatically become the property of the publishers and will not be returned. The decision of the *Earls Courtier* in selecting the winning entry will be final, and no correspondence will be entered into.

Entries should be addressed to the *Earls Courtier*, 20 Notting Hill Gate, London, W.11, and should be marked "Short Story Competition". Your own name and address should be clearly shown.

A group of overseas visitors at the newly opened trattoria "Il Palio di Siena" at 133 Earls Court Road, S.W.5.

ITALY COMES TO EARLS COURT

BY M. WHITE

THE vogue for trattoria—literally, in Italian, eating house—has become firmly established in this country and in London has been creeping from Soho, where it started, to east, west, north, and south of Piccadilly. Most westerly is that recently opened in Earls Court Road named "Il Palio di Siena". Its owner, Mr. Celio Birindelli, has unique experience as a restaurateur having been at the Versailles in Soho and at the Berkeley, Piccadilly. He hails from a small village outside Florence, where his family has its own vineyards which produce wines which are drunk with dishes of typically Italian origin in which, of course, Celio's restaurant specialises. Celio tells me that he has a surprise for his customers, many of whom are drawn from the colony of overseas visitors who form a considerable percentage of the Earls Court population. (See photograph above). When he shortly opens a third salon at Earls Court Road I can give you a hint of his intentions—the introduction of a completely new dish of his own invention.

INTERSKY CLUB BRINGS NEW LOOK TO TOURISM

FOR the tourist to know that with every mile he or she travels they are making money must be unique. Yet this is what membership of the newly-formed Intersky puts within reach of the intending traveller. Membership of Intersky is synonymous with partnership. Member-shareholders in the enterprise not only enjoy the privilege of "cut" rates in the cost of their itinerary—and this can cover almost every quarter of the globe—but they receive a dividend as well. Virtually they are part and parcel of the organisation and are entitled to a vote in its management. There are even *FREE* flights for life members. Life membership costs R1080 which can be paid by instalments. Ordinary members can obtain flights at cost price. Ordinary membership costs R130. Economical luxury mini-bus vacations in South Africa and other parts of the world are an annual feature.

SRI LANKA RESTAURANT
FULLY LICENCED
CEYLONESE · FOOD
INDIAN, PAKISTANI and CONTINENTAL DISHES
Open 12 noon to 3 p.m. 6 p.m. till midnight
SPECIAL ORDERS—TWELVE HOUR NOTICE
19 CHILDS STREET, EARLS COURT, S.W.5.
Prop. J. C. SILVA
FRE. 4116

OVERLAND INDIA – AUSTRALIA
TRAVEL SENSIBLY BY "INDIAMAN"
THE ORIGINAL—THE EXPERIENCED—THE DEPENDABLE TOUR
AUSTRALIA—NEW ZEALAND
Specialists Air—Sea—Road
WHY NOT ASK!
GARROW-FISHER TOURS
(opposite Railway Station)
56 WOOD ST., KINGSTON
KIN. 2913

LE SOUS SOL
THE PAD WITH THE ATMOSPHERE
117 Earls Court Road, S.W.5
FRE 0518

H. FENTON (HAIRDRESSERS) LTD.
167 EARLS COURT ROAD, S.W.5
for GENTLEMEN'S EXPERT HAIRCUTTING
4 Assistants in Attendance
No Waiting

Printed by Wiltshire Printing Co. (Croydon) Ltd., 131 Love Lane, Mitcham, Surrey. For the Publishers The Earls Courtier, 20 Notting Hill Gate, W.11.

14. *The presence of Australian, New Zealand and South African residents in Earl's Court, is reflected in this special newspaper issued in September 1992.*

to where the Science Museum is. To their south, along the Cromwell Road, stood – for barely two years – an exhibition building even larger than the famed 'Crystal Palace' of 1851. The Kensington Canal was filled in over a century and a half ago. Earl's Court's Great Wheel, a predecessor of the London Eye, survived little more than a decade.

Much that has survived has been transformed virtually beyond recognition. Bonham's present building actually encases the Brompton Chapel, opened for local needs in 1768. In 1871 it was described as "simply ugly outside and very little more may be said of it inside". In 1888 it was converted to become a church school, which survived until 1939.

The transformations have been even more dramatic socially than physically. When it was built in the 1830s Pelham Place was almost entirely inhabited by humble cabmen. Just over a century later stylish royal photographer Cecil Beaton would be standing at the doorway of No. 8, side by side with the critic Cyril Connolly, looking out on Blitz-battered London – an "apricot haze" glimpsed through "blue vistas of Watteauesque trees". Beaton, like Brompton, survived the war only slightly knocked about, to re-establish a graciousness of living in serene surroundings. A quarter of a century after his early evening vigil with Connolly, Beaton was once again entertaining him to dinner in company with the formidable Martita Hunt, the very personification of Wilde's Lady Bracknell. The evening began cautiously but ended in a whirlwind of wit and thespian reminiscence. This minor social triumph was subsequently overshadowed by Beaton hosting a lunch for the Queen Mother at which the other guests included Truman Capote and Edith Sitwell. When this occasion was repeated, as an even greater success, the guests included the then V & A director Roy Strong, veteran American actress Irene Worth, legendary society beauty, hostess and writer Lady Diana Cooper – and the Queen. The peculiar genius of the locality may be that only in such a setting could such an assemblage seem quite *natural*.

15. Hale House, south of Cromwell Road on a site now covered by Queen's Gate. It was once owned by William Methwold, who built the almshouses depicted in illusration 16.

Rural Retreats

Eighteenth century Kensington, though still largely covered with fields, orchards, nurseries and market gardens, also had a dozen or so substantial villas which served as places of refreshment or retirement to persons of eminence – or at least affluence.

The site of Hale House, which dated from at least the sixteenth century, is now completely covered by the roadway of Queen's Gate, just south of its junction with Cromwell Road. In 1606 Hale House was bought by Sir William Blake (died 1630), a London vintner, who built up substantial holdings throughout the Kensington area. In 1645 the purchaser was William Methwold, who eventually became Deputy Governor of the East India Company. He built Methwold's Almshouses at the southern end of his property to house six poor women. Following Methwold's demise Hale House was let to a succession of tenants, the most distinguished of whom was the statesman Edmund Burke. He took it in 1794 to recover the health of an ailing son, who nevertheless died there. The house was finally demolished in 1853, the almshouses twenty years later.

Brompton Park House, which stood at the south-west corner of what is now the site of the Victoria and Albert Museum, was, for forty years, the home of royal gardener Henry Wise. It may then have become a girls' boarding-school (*see p. 67*). In 1784 it was converted into a terrace of three properties but this implied no social degradation as the residents included the Dowager Countess of Warwick, a judge and an earl. In the mid-nineteenth century the buildings were absorbed into the South Kensington Museum complex to become art school accommodation and finally demolished in 1899 as part of Sir Aston Webb's general rebuilding scheme.

Short-lived Gloucester Lodge (originally Orford Lodge) stood approximately opposite the present day Gloucester Road station and was built on the site of the failed pleasure-ground known as Florida Gardens (*see p.31*). When architect William Tyler exhibited his plans for the new mansion at the Royal Academy in 1800 its location, on a meandering artery known as Hogmire Lane sounded, perhaps, just a trifle too rustic. The name was changed to Gloucester Road in compliment to the first occupant – Maria, Duchess of Gloucester, sister-in-law of King George III. Her successor as occupant, from 1809 to 1825, was Tory politician George Canning

16. Methwold's Almshouses near Queen's Gate, with St Augustine's church being built in the background. Illustration by C.J. Richardson in 1871.

17. Brompton Park House with the dome of the 1862 International Exhibition building in the background. Painting by R. Collinson, 1862.

(1770-1827). An aristocrat by birth, educated at Eton and Christ Church and an MP at 24, Canning solved the inconvenience of his personal impecuniousness by marrying an heiress worth £100,000. Foreign Secretary at 37, he resigned the year he moved into Gloucester Lodge following a quarrel with his bitter rival Castlereagh. The quarrel ended in a duel in which Canning was wounded in the leg. He did not return to office until 1818. In 1822, following Castlereagh's suicide, Canning once again became Foreign Secretary, fostering the independence of Spain's former colonies in South America and supporting the Greek struggle aganst Turkish overlordship. In 1827 he served briefly as Prime Minister following the death of Lord Liverpool, but the strain of office undermined his health within months. Canning was noted in youth for his witty versifying, in maturity for an oratory that was so outstanding in diction, language and reasoning that he was even praised by Byron:

> Even thy genius, Canning, may permit,
> Who, bred a statesman, still was born a wit,
> And never, even in that dull House, could'st tame
> To unleaven'd prose thine own poetic flame;
> Our last, our best, our only orator.

Canning was, however, severely handicapped in his career by a deserved reputation as an ambitious adventurer and by class hostility against his parentage, his father having died in penury, his mother having been an actress. He was, nevertheless, buried in Westminster Abbey. His statue stands at the Great George Street corner of Parliament Square. Gloucester Lodge was demolished in 1851, having stood for just half a century.

THE GORE HOUSE SAGA

Gore House once stood at Kensington Gore, occupying what is now the site of Albert Hall Mansions. Built in the 1750s, in 1784 it became the retirement home of the celebrated Admiral Rodney (1719-92). Entering the navy at thirteen, Rodney had become a captain at twenty-three and a rear-admiral at forty. Despite a career of profitable actions, he had been financially ruined by his weakness for women, extravagant socialising and dabbling in politics but all seemed gloriously redeemed at a stroke following his destruction of a Spanish fleet off Cape St Vincent in 1780. Awarded a knighthood and the Freedom of the City, Rodney fought a Caribbean campaign which gained him a peerage and a pension but left him cursed by acrimonious relations

18. Gloucester Lodge, located opposite today's Gloucester Road Underground station, built on the site of the Florida Gardens pleasure ground. It was demolished in 1851.

19. Gore House, on the site of today's Albert Hall Mansions, was home to William Wilberforce and the Countess of Blessington.

with brother officers and encumbered with law suits. To these in retirement at Gore House he added the agonies of acute gout.

From 1808 to 1821 Gore House was the home of celebrated parliamentarian and philanthropist William Wilberforce (1759-1833), by then venerated as "the authorised interpreter of the national conscience". Born to wealth, clever, charming, a fine singer, a wicked mimic and open-handed to a fault, Wilberforce became an MP at twenty-one and a lifelong friend of William Pitt soon after. In his twenties Wilberforce underwent a spiritual rejuvenation, akin to reconversion, which set him on a high moral path without turning him into a puritan. In 1787 Wilberforce recorded in his journal that "God Almighty has set before me two great objects, the suppression of the Slave Trade and the reformation of manners".

He campaigned against pornography, was instrumental in establishing the Church Missionary Society and in 1797 published a handbook, *Practical Christianity*, which went through

20. William Wilberforce, social reformer and anti-slavery campaigner.

21. Marguerite, the Countess of Blessington – a hostess who spent the mostest.

fifteen editions in less than twenty years. It took two decades of tireless propaganda and parliamentary manoeuvring for Wilberforce to secure the abolition of the slave trade in 1807. The strain on his health was such that in the following year he left Clapham in favour of Kensington where he could be nearer the House of Commons, yet still enjoy the delights of a garden full of "lilacs, laburnums, nightingales and swallows". Wilberforce kept open house and received a constant stream of visitors until once again increasing frailty forced another move, this time to "a little property of 140 acres" at Mill Hill. Mrs Wilberforce, who had found the open house policy a great strain on her powers of domestic organisation, was doubtless much relieved.

A decade after Wilberforce moved out, Gore House became the residence of Marguerite, Countess of Blessington (1789-1849), who proceeded to make its library the focus of London's most brilliant literary and social salon. Lady Blessington's own colourful life would have made her an ideal heroine for a Georgette Heyer romance and doubtless provided much material for her own literary productions, such as *The Victims of Society* and *Confessions of an Elderly Lady*. Irish by birth and, by misfortune, the daughter of an irascible, dissolute dandy, Marguerite was married off to a worthless Captain Farmer when she was only fourteen and a half. Farmer eventually liberated her from the unwanted bonds of matrimony by falling out of a window and killing himself when dead drunk. In the meantime Marguerite, initially the only plain child in a strikingly handsome family, had blossomed into a beauty so stunning that she was painted by Sir Thomas Lawrence himself. Marrying the spendthrift Earl of Blessington, whose Irish holdings brought him £30,000 a year, brought Marguerite a title, a jointure, a house in St James's Square, the leisure to essay a little anonymous authorship and the opportunity to undertake a seven-year Grand Tour of Europe which ended only with her husband's death. En route she met Byron, who deemed her "highly literary ... [and] very pretty even in a morning". She also gathered an entourage which included the future comic actor Charles Mathews and the Count D'Orsay, a French army officer, who resigned his commission, married Blessington's fifteen-year-old daughter, separated from her almost immediately and became Marguerite's lifelong companion thereafter. D'Orsay, a charming six-foot Adonis, who could paint and sculpt as well, completed 125 profile sketches of the celebrities who thronged Gore House but made little material contribution to its expenses. The death of the Earl having left Marguerite in reduced circumstances, she applied both industry and intellect to the task of authorship. Gossip pieces, beauty hints and novels of high society shenanigans brought in up to £3,000 a year, which was a goodly income – unless you happened to be spending £4,000 a year. Ironically it was the Irish famine which hastened the inevitable smash. By 1848 Marguerite's jointure had dwindled to nothing. On 1 April 1849 D'Orsay made fools of his creditors by fleeing to Paris with his valet and a single portmanteau. Marguerite joined him a fortnight later. An auction of what they abandoned drew 20,000 visitors and raised £12,000 against their debts. Marguerite died a month later in the home of D'Orsay's sister. He died, mourned by his friend the newly-crowned emperor Napoleon III in 1852, and was buried beside her in the mausoleum he had erected to her memory.

One final chapter remained in the roller-coaster history of Gore House. Alexis Soyer (1809-58) might, perhaps, fairly be claimed as Britain's first 'celebrity cook'. As chef of the Reform Club he had pioneered the use of gas in cooking, with hi-tech ovens that became one of the capital's more offbeat visitor attractions. Soyer married a beautiful and talented artist, wrote cookbooks for both rich and poor, sponsored soup-kitchens during the Irish famine and made a fortune out of a table-top spirit-stove of his own devising. The prospect of millions of visitors thronging to Prince Albert's proclaimed Great Exhibition in 1851 inspired him with the seductive and glittering vision of opening a top-line restaurant in Gore House, which stood immediately over the way from the Exhibition itself. 'Soyer's Gastronomic Symposium of All Nations' occupied not only the house but, complemented by a 'Baronial Banqueting Hall' and a 'Pavilion of All Nations' four hundred feet long, took up most of the grounds as well. The opening was a huge success, press coverage being vigorously orchestrated by the youthful George Sala (*see p. 116*), an enthusiastic backer of the project. The daring venture brought in £21,000 – but cost £28,000. Following this commercially farcical flourish Gore House was finally torn down in 1857.

In the same year nearby Grove House, which stood on the site of the Albert Hall, was also erased. Sir Caesar Hawkins (1711-86), who had lived there from 1749 to 1764, was the son of a country doctor. Appointed surgeon at St George's Hospital when only twenty-four, he remained in post there for just short of forty years, also serving successively as surgeon to the Prince of Wales and then as Sergeant-Surgeon to George II and George III. Anne Pitt, sister of the Earl of Chatham, followed him as tenant and prettified the place noticeably, possibly with the assistance of Robert Adam. Then came another medical man, Sir John Elliott (1736-86), surgeon to the future George IV, to whom he attempted to preach the value of temperance – in vain. In 1771 Elliott married Grace Dalrymple, who was scarcely out of puberty. When she eloped with Lord Valentia, Elliott, already a rich man, gained not only a divorce but £12,000 damages as well. Elliott appears not to have been overly damaged by the episode, receiving a baronetcy in 1778. From 1816 to 1846 Grove House was occupied by Lady Elizabeth Whitbread, widow of the outspoken reforming MP and staunch ally of Wilberforce, Samuel Whitbread; he had cut his own throat in July 1815.

Fancifully named Eden Lodge, which stood where the Royal Geographical Society now stands at the corner of Exhibition Road, was around 1745 occupied by John Swinhoe, then owner of

22. Cowper House Lunatic Asylum on the Old Brompton Road. Built in the 18th century, it was an asylum from 1829 until its demolition in 1850. The inhabitants are shown enjoying a therapeutic game of cricket.

23. Grove House, also known as Brompton Place, on the Old Brompton Road, nearly opposite today's South Kensington Underground station.

the Brompton Park Nursery. A century later it was the home of the Earl of Auckland, returned from serving as Governor-General of India. Eden Lodge was finally pulled down in the early 1870s.

ALONG OLD BROMPTON ROAD

Cowper House (*ill. 22*), so named for a nineteenth century occupant Henry Cowper, stood on the south side of Old Brompton Road on the site now occupied by Melton Court. A house was built here by Robert Sewell in the early seventeenth century and rebuilt by Samuel Bucknall in the eighteenth century. Cowper House was used as a private lunatic asylum from 1829 until its demolition in 1850. A contemporary print shows inmates playing cricket beside the long avenue of elms which once stretched through its grounds down to the Fulham Road. Their line is echoed in the replanted double row of trees in the eastern part of Onslow Square gardens.

Grove House, also known as Brompton Place, once stood on the north side of Old Brompton Road, more or less opposite where South Kensington station now stands, and was built between 1720 and 1740. Its most famous resident was Sir John Fielding (1721-80), half-brother of Henry Fielding, the author of *Tom Jones*. Despite his blindness, Sir John continued the novelist's crusade as a Bow Street magistrate to smash the gangs of thieves which plagued the streets of the metropolis. In this the 'Blind Beak' seems to have been far from scrupulous in his methods, though he did try to turn younger culprits onto a better path by sending them to sea rather than the gallows. Knighted for his services in 1761, Fielding moved to Grove House in 1768, dying there in 1780.

Forty years later Grove House became the residence of William Jerdan (1782-1869), who had lived in the Brompton area since 1808. A Scot, restless for literary recognition, he made a shaky start as a journalist in London, being associated with a sequence of failed publications. He did, however, make the friendship of that other local adventurer, George Canning (*see p. 16*), became a regular guest at Gloucester Lodge and had his neighbour stand godfather to one of his children. Jerdan also achieved fortuitous distinction as an eyewitness to the murder of Prime Minister Spencer Perceval in 1812 and further distinguished himself by apprehending the deranged assassin, Bellingham. Jerdan finally found his métier as editor of the newly-

24. A large mansion on Old Brompton Road, probably Brompton Hall before its Victorian restoration. Methwold's Almshouses are to the right.

25. A 1749 newspaper cutting relating to Brompton Hall. It notifies the public that this recently restored house is now converted for the reception of 'Persons afflicted with Nervous Disorders'. It goes on to say that Brompton is remarkable for its mild, warm Air, and therefore peculiarly favourable to 'Hypochondriack Cases'.

THE Publick are desired to be informed, that the *Great White House*, with all its Offices, commonly called *Brumpton-Hall*, (lately in the Possession of Edmund Jenkins, Esq;) pleasantly situated in a fine, soft, healthy Air, adjoining two delightful extensive Gardens, compleatly walled, furnished and adorned with a beautiful Variety of Ever-Greens, Flowers, Fruit-Trees, a Summer-House, Grass-Plats, and Gravel Walks, &c. is newly repaired in a most inviting Manner, for the commodious Reception of *Persons afflicted with Nervous Complaints*, and attended by a Physician of long Experience in those Disorders, having practised upwards of thirty Years in this City, and can satisfactorily be recommended by Persons of undoubted Veracity and Distinction, who desire to attest many signal Cures performed by his Prescriptions; and on that account themselves have encouraged him to purchase the said House, in order to accommodate his Patients therewith, his House in Town being too confined of late by the new Buildings.

But what the Publick are in particular to be ecquainted with is, *Brumpton* is remarkable for a mild, warm Air, and therefore must be peculiarly favourable to the *Hypochondriack Cases*, and much contributory to a speedy Cure. And what renders this House more engaging is, that notwithstanding it is but better than one Mile from Town, and Half a one from Kensington, yet it is as private, retired, and rural, as if it were more than 50 or 60 Miles off.

*** Relating to further Particulars, enquire at the said House.

founded *Literary Gazette* (1817-62), which he swiftly raised to eminence, recruiting an able stable of reviewers and contributors. In 1821 Jerdan was instrumental in founding the Royal Society of Literature and later played a similar role with respect to the Royal Geographical Society, the Garrick Club and the Camden Society. He was also elected F.S.A. In 1826, however, he made severe losses in a banking crash and was subsequently destroyed in the 1840s when defrauded by a friend to whom he had entrusted his remaining capital. In 1850 Jerdan was forced to sell Grove House and move to Bushey Heath where he continued to write indefatigably, relying on the slender support of a Civil List pension.

Further west but still towards the eastern end of Old Brompton Road, to the east of Methwold's almshouses, stood Bute House, built by Scottish architect James Adam (1730-94) for his own occupation around 1770. He sold it in 1782. Adam was the younger brother of Robert Adam and is usually credited with laying out Portland Place, then the widest street in London, in 1773. Adam also had literary interests, having published an account of travels in Italy and a treatise on agriculture. At the time of his death he was working on a history of architecture. From 1795 to 1804 the house was occupied by the first

26. Anna Maria Hall, resident at The Rosary; a studio portrait of c.1860.

Marquess of Bute. It was demolished in 1846.

To the east of Bute House on the north side of Old Brompton Road stood Brompton Hall (*ills 24 & 25*). Dating back to the sixteenth century, it was demolished in 1874.

Further to the west, beyond where the line of Gloucester Road now forms an intersection, were four more residences, built around the 1760s and demolished in the 1880s and known, from east to west respectively, as The Rosary, Hereford Lodge, Clareville and Brompton Villa.

The most celebrated resident of The Rosary, the site of which is now covered by Rosary Gardens, was Anna Maria Hall (née Fielding) (1800-81) who lived there from 1839 to 1849 with her husband, the architect and editor of the *New Monthly Magazine*, S. C. Hall, who may be the model for the odious Mr Pecksniff in Dickens' *Martin Chuzzlewit*. Mrs Hall's own prolific literary output ranged from sketches of Irish life to stage plays, children's stories, travel guides, moralising tales in the cause of temperance and nine novels. Her work was never popular in her native Ireland, perhaps because she offended Orangemen and Catholics equally by finding

27. The Rosary, near the junction of Old Brompton Road and Gloucester Road, has given its name to Rosary Gardens.

virtues as well as shortcomings in both communities. A devout Christian, she championed the cause of street musicians and was instrumental in founding the Brompton Hospital, the Governesses' Institution and the Home for Decayed Gentlewomen.

In 1798 Hereford Lodge was the home of soprano Gertrud Elizabeth Mara (née Schmeling) (1749-1833). Born in Cassel, she was the daughter of an impoverished musician who anticipated Leopold Mozart by touring her as a prodigy violinist. Her talent as a singer became apparent in London in 1759. She subsequently accepted a well-paid post at the court of Frederick the Great of Prussia, only to flee his bullying and live intermittently in London between 1792 and 1802. Her marriage to the cellist Mara proved disastrous, though she stuck by him despite his violence, extravagance and dissipation, which wasted her resources so much that she was reduced to teaching in Russia, where Napoleon's sack of Moscow completed her ruin. An attempt to recover her fortunes by a surprise return to the London concert platform at the age of sixty-eight ended in total humiliation as her voice had by then quite gone. Hereford Lodge subsequently housed a Sunday School and a photographic printing company before its final demise. Clareville also had musical associations through the temporary residence of Jenny Lind on her early visits to London in 1848 and 1849.

Brompton Villa was a spacious accommodation with nine bedrooms and a range of outbuildings which included a cowhouse and piggeries. Between 1817 and 1820 it was the home of poet Laetitia Landon (1802-38). Born and educated in Hans Place (*see p. 68*), she was a naturally bookish girl of lively intelligence who attracted the

28. Clareville in the Old Brompton Road, for a short time the residence of the singer, Jenny Lind.

attention of William Jerdan. Her first published poem appeared in his *Literary Gazette* in 1820. S.C. Hall was also among her admirers. Laetitia became a prolific contributor of poems and sketches to magazines under the pseudonym L.E.L. Although she earned an estimated £2,500 she was pressurised by the demands of a genteel family anxious to escape a penury stretching back to the South Sea Bubble of 1720. Rumour, doubtless baseless, linked her scandalously with the febrile Irish writer William Maginn, a fellow contributor to Jerdan's publication, and caused her to break off her engagement with John Forster, Dickens' friend. On the rebound she married George Maclean, governor of Cape Coast Castle and sailed for South Africa with him. Shortly after her arrival she died of prussic acid poisoning; whether it was suicide, an accident or the revenge of a discarded mistress remained unclear.

Between Old Brompton Road and Fulham Road, west of Drayton Gardens, once stood Coleherne House, on the site now occupied by Coleherne Court (*see p. 13*). A house was certainly on the site in 1647 when Cromwell's right-hand man and most successful general, John Lambert, attended a christening there. Between about 1705 and 1721 it was the home of Sir Richard Blackmore (1654-1729), physician to William III and Queen Anne but better remembered for his literary efforts, which ranged from theology to medicine to poetry of inordinate length. Ridiculed by Dryden and Pope, he won the praise of Addison for his *Creation; a philosophical Poem demonstrating the Existence and Providence of God* (1712). Johnson included Blackmore in his *Lives of the Poets* series and wrote of *Creation* that "if he had written nothing else [it] would have transmitted him to posterity as one of the first favourites of the English Muse." The property was bought by Philip Gilbert in 1810 and rebuilt as Hereford Lodge (demolished 1900). The occupants of Hereford Lodge included the burlesque writer Charles Dance (1841-5) and the theatrical managers Benjamin Lumley (1857-9) and Dion Boucicault.

29. Coleherne House, between Old Brompton Road and Fulham Road. Coleherne Court stands on its site.

30. Cromwell's general, John Lambert, who attended a christening at Coleherne House.

EARL'S COURT

Earl's Court House, demolished in 1886 to make way for the building of Barkston Gardens, was from 1765 until his death the extraordinary home of pioneering anatomist John Hunter (1728-93). Hunter's house was on the site of a handsome mansion once occupied by Secretary of the Treasury Henry Guy in the 1690s. Its garden had been noted for its walks and waterworks, fountains and luxurious tiled and marble-paved dairy and bath-house. In Hunter's time the garden seems to have been more like a combination of jungle and farmyard than a restful suburban refuge. Feckless as a child in his native Scotland, he had but a poor schooling and worked at first as an assistant to a brother, cabinet-making. Another brother, William (1718-73) called him south to assist him in the task of dissecting corpses, for which he readily showed a positive genius. Hunter compensated for his lack of formal qualifications by gaining bloody practical experience of anatomy through service with the military during the Seven Years War, laying the groundwork of a lifetime's interest in the treatment of gunshot wounds (and venereal diseases). He built up a lucrative private practice, despite refusing, as a matter of principle, fees from any curate, author or artist. For Hunter, the menag-

31. Earl's Court House pictured in 1870 when in use as a private lunatic asylum. It was demolished to make way for Barkston Gardens.

erie in his Earl's Court garden substituted for a library. He obtained the privilege of first refusal on exotic beasts which expired at the Tower of London and over his lifetime spent an estimated £10,000 accumulating a collection of 13,600 stuffed specimens and skeletons which, after his death, eventually passed to the Royal College of Surgeons. It was truly said of Hunter's educational grounding that few men have started with so little to do so much. Subsequent inhabitants of Earl's Court House included Lord Byron's family solicitor, John Hanson and a mistress of the Duke of Richmond. From 1832 until 1878 it served as a private mad-house for ladies of the affluent classes.

South of Hunter's home stood Earl's Court Lodge on a site now covered by the YWCA at 227 Earl's Court Road. From 1797 to 1857 this was the family home of the Gunters, who made a fortune out of market-gardening, confectionery and catering before decamping to Yorkshire and turning their local estate over to development (*see p. 42*). From 1899 to 1909 the building, then known as Park House, was occupied by Madame Albani and her impresario husband (*see p. 91*). It was finally knocked down to make way for a YWCA hostel in 1921; this was itself replaced in 1973.

32. The anatomist, John Hunter.

Gardens and Nurseries

THE NURSERIES

Brompton Park Nursery was founded in 1681 by George London (died 1714), Moses Cook, gardener to the Earl of Essex ,and two other leading gardeners, Roger Looker and John Field. In 1687 Field died and Henry Wise (1653-1738) joined the partnership. By 1689 Looker had died and Cook had sold out, so control passed entirely to London and his sole remaining partner Henry Wise. Their talents were complementary, London being the plantsman and designer, Wise the administrator and businessman. London habitually took to the saddle to ride as far as Yorkshire to deal with provincial clients. Wise kept close connections with the royal court and managed the nursery as the essential base of their operations. The enterprise they built up together lasted, under successive changes of ownership, until 1852, when it closed after finally trading as Gray, Adams and Hogg.

At its height Brompton Park Nursery stretched over a hundred acres, being the first, and for long the largest, commercial nursery in the metropolis. The diarist John Evelyn, himself a connoisseur of gardens, recorded taking a friend to see it in April 1694: "I carried Mr. Waller to see Brompton-park, where he was in admiration at the store of rare plants and the method he found in that noble nursery ...". Essayist and social commentator Joseph Addison was another admirer, hailing London and Wise as 'our heroick Poets' of gardening. Bowack's *Antiquities of Middlesex* (1705-6) described the nursery as an institution of national importance – "famed all over the kingdom ... brought to its greatest perfection and kept in extraordinary order, in which a great number of men are constantly employed. The stock seems almost incredible, for if we believe some who affirm that the several plants in it were valued at but a 1d. they would amount to above £40,000."

George London's origins are so obscure that neither the date nor the place of his birth are known. He trained under the happily named royal gardener John Rose (died 1677), who had himself trained under Andre Le Notre, designer of the gardens at Versailles. Rose obtained

33. *Greenwood's map of 1830, showing the central area of Brompton given over to nurseries.*

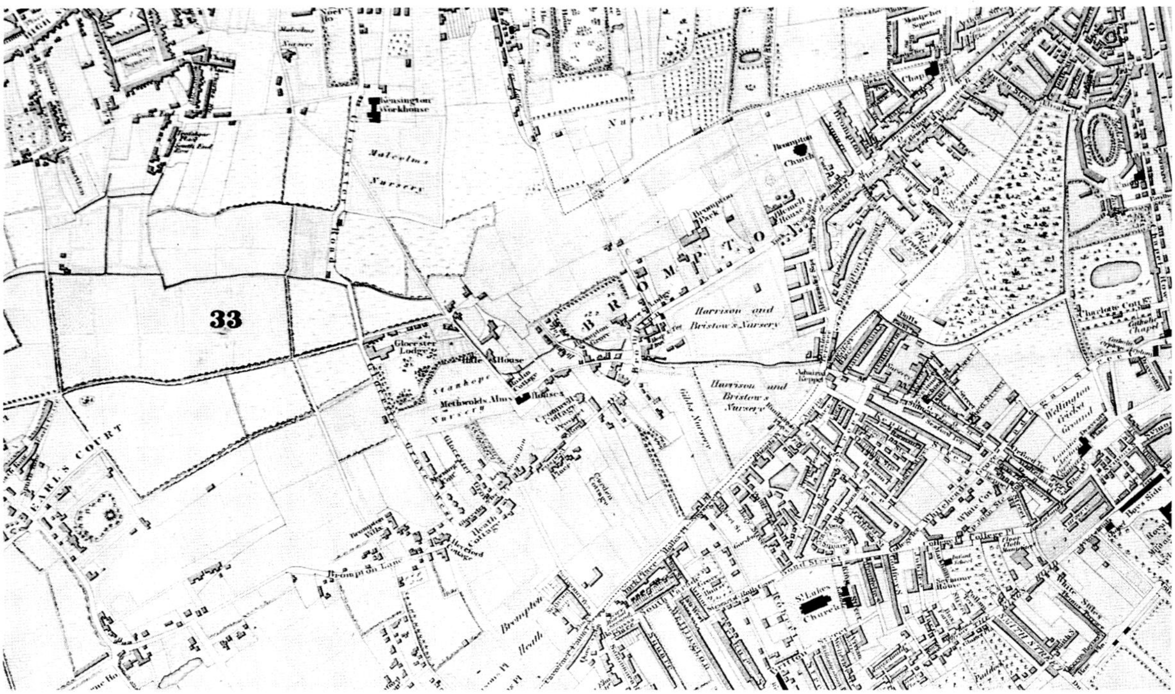

employment for George London with Henry Compton (1675-1713), the bishop of London, himself another keen gardener. The prelate's summer retreat, Fulham Palace, benefited from his subsidiary role as bishop to the American colonies, in which capacity he received such exotic new imports as the first magnolia. Fulham Palace garden became therefore a major conduit for the importation of novel plant varieties to Britain, many of its contents being auctioned off to competing nurserymen at the time of Compton's death. By then London and Wise had forged a close and mutually profitable relationship with royal architect William Talman. This brought them not only commissions at Kensington Palace, Windsor Castle, Hampton Court, Chelsea Hospital and St James's Park, but also at such prestigious provincial venues as Longleat, Chatsworth, Blenheim and Castle Howard. Their work at Wanstead House, on the eastern fringe of the metropolis, was considered a particular triumph, compared by contemporaries to Versailles itself. The comparison was not overly fanciful. London had studied French gardens at first-hand, had met the great Le Notre himself and was a confident and imaginative constructor of parterres and waterworks.

After London's death, Wise sold up to concentrate on consultancy and the maintenance of royal palace gardens but continued to live in Brompton Park House. He outlived London by almost a quarter of a century, served as Royal Gardener to three successive monarchs and died in his native Warwickshire, allegedly worth the fabulous sum of £200,000.

Almost all of the gardens laid out by London and Wise have long since disappeared. A number were drastically altered by the next generation of garden-designers, reacting against their formalism and in favour of a more naturalistic landscape look. Leading the trend were two of their own trainees at Brompton – Charles Bridgeman (died 1738) who succeeded Wise as Royal Gardener in 1728 and Stephen Switzer (1682-1745), author of an influential treatise *The Nobleman, Gentleman and Gardener's Recreation* (1715). The most enduring legacy of London and Wise was, therefore, Brompton Park Nursery itself. An anonymous but clearly educated 'labourer employed in Mr. Wise's garden at Brompton' paid a handsome and witty tribute in verse:

If he who the first garden made
Had put in Wise to keep it,
Made Adam but a labourer there
And Eve to weed and sweep it;
Then men and plants had never died,
Nor the first fruits been rotten;
Brompton had never then been known
Nor Eden e'er forgotten.

The nursery established by Robert Furber (?1674-1756) at Kensington Gore in 1700 remained in business, latterly under one Richard Forrest, until 1846 and was as remarkable for its marketing techniques as for its range of exotic stock, much of which was also derived from Fulham Palace at Bishop Compton's demise. In 1730 Furber commissioned Flemish artist Pieter Casteels (1684-1749) to engrave a dozen plates illustrating *Twelve Months of Flowers*, subsequently published with commentary as *The Flower Garden Display'd* and followed by *Twelve Months of Fruit* (*see ill. 34*). The illustration for May shows how far assiduous plant-hunters had fostered an industry that was already global in its sources of supply, featuring Venetian Vetch, Dwarf Dutch Tulip, China Pink, Virginian Colombine, Red Austrian Rose and Blew Hyacinth of Peru. These plates not only served as a catalogue of the four hundred varieties which Furber regularly carried – and an indirect indication of the elite nature of his clientele – but, as Furber observed in an accompanying preface would be "very useful not only for the curious in gardening but the Prints likewise for Painters, Carvers, Japaners etc. also for the Ladies, as Patterns for Working and Painting in water-Colours; or Furniture for the Closet". Furber, like Wise, was a member of the Society of Gardeners, a study-group led by Philip Miller, superintendent of the Chelsea Physick Garden, which met to exchange experience and to tackle such technical questions as the regularisation of nomenclature for new varieties. That Furber was locally a man of consequence can be inferred from the fact that he served both as an overseer of the poor and a churchwarden at St Mary Abbot's, where he was buried.

Around 1750 an extensive nursery was established by Henry and Samuel Hewitt, covering the area which subsequently became the Alexander estate – Alexander Square, Thurloe Square and the adjacent streets. By 1790 ownership had devolved through a series of partnership changes to John Harrison. The business specialised in

34. August 1732, a plate from 'Twelve Months of Fruit', issued by Robert Furber using plates made by Flemish artist Pieter Casteels (see p.29)

fruit trees, seeds and greenhouse plants. In 1815 John Harrison passed the business to his brother Samuel, who enlarged it by some eight extra acres. In 1830 Samuel became the first tenant of 12 Alexander Square but was forced to vacate it in 1832 when he went bankrupt, forfeiting a lease on the nursery good for another ten years. This enabled development of the area to go forward earlier than had been envisaged.

Another run of nurseries was located along the line of the Fulham Road. Coming from London the first was one still in the hands of Thomas Gibbs as late as 1841. Gibbs was seedsman and nurseryman to the Board of Agriculture and had a shop at the corner of Half Moon Street, Piccadilly. His Fulham Road enterprise was essentially an experimental station, divided into small plots for testing strains of grasses, root crops and grains.

A nursery run by one Richard Selwood stood on the site of the Brompton Hospital (*see p. 44*) as early as the seventeenth century. By the mid-eighteenth century, under John / Jean Rubergall, it was celebrated for its lettuces. In 1789 the tenancy passed to William Curtis (1746-99), an important figure in the history of gardening. Trained as an apothecary and initially employed as a demonstrator of practical botany to medical students, Curtis established his first botanical garden at Bermondsey before moving it to Lambeth in 1779 and then a decade later to Brompton. Curtis established his scientific reputation with publications on entomology and then in 1777 confirmed it with his study of the plant life of the capital, *Flora Londiniensis*. Curtis was also a founder member of the Linnaean Society and publisher of *The Botanical Magazine*. Curtis's Brompton Botanical Gardens was supported by subscribers who were given rights of admission with guests and the privilege of buying surplus seeds and cuttings. The exhibition gardens extended over almost exactly the three and a half acres subsequently covered by the Brompton Hospital and adjacent streets, while the four and a half acres lying immediately to the north were used for experimental plantings. After Curtis's early death from a heart condition his partner William Salisbury moved the garden to Chelsea but kept the Brompton holding on as a nursery until 1829, when it became David Ramsay's Swan Lane nursery. His son, David Allan Ramsay, eventually vacated the area to make way for the construction of the hospital.

The firm of Wills and Segar (*ill. 37*) was established by John Wills in Onslow Crescent in the 1860s and prospered mightily from the contemporary craze for indoor floral decoration and conservatories. By 1880 the business had become incorporated as a limited company. It also gained a Royal Warrant. Much of its ground was covered with glasshouses, its major speciality being palms, ferns and other ornamental foliage plants.

35. William Curtis, a man renowned for his knowledge of bugs, botany and business

FLORIDA GARDENS

By the mid-eighteenth century pleasure gardens had become a notable feature of London's leisure scene. Their purposes and activities were various, from taking tea against a soothing background of music to less innocent pleasures. The largest and most famous were at Ranelagh and Vauxhall, on either side of the Thames, but there were dozens more smaller ones, notably in Clerkenwell and Marylebone. Their common features were accessibility from a fashionable residential area and at least a semi-rural setting. Florida Gardens, sited on what is now Stanhope Gardens, outside Gloucester Road station, answered both requirements. Established at least as early as 1762, it flourished in the following

36. Florida Gardens, a popular London pleasure ground in the 1780s and 1790s. This view, artist unknown, was executed c.1827-30. The site is now taken by Stanhope Gardens.

decade thanks doubtless in part to what a contemporary referred to as a "retired situation ... well adapted for gallantry and intrigue". By 1769 the proprietor was a German florist and gardener, Rudolf Heim, who used part of the property to cultivate flowers, strawberries and cherries. In particular he pioneered the growing of monster Grafton cherries, allegedly up to four inches in circumference. He converted from being a florist to a confectioner *c.*1776. The pleasure garden side of the business was up-graded by the addition of a bowling-green and a 'Long Room' capable of accommodating five hundred. The attractions were diversified by the engagement of an orchestra and the arrangement of a programme of firework displays, balloon ascents and displays of horsemanship. Visitors could also admire amusing topiary figures of birds and animals and, for a modest charge, pick flowers and fruit from the nursery to carry home with them. Heim's glory was short-lived and he was bankrupted in the 1790s. The land was bought in 1797 and built over by the widowed Duchess of Gloucester, who called her new home Orford Lodge (*see p. 16*) and lived in it until her death in 1807.

37. The premises of Wills and Segar in Onslow Crescent, by then much reduced, in 1934.

The Brompton Estates

From 1726 what is now the Brompton Road was a major turnpike leading westwards out of the metropolis. Its most immediately noticeable features were public houses, a number clustered at its eastern end, others strung out further along the route. Their presence is explained by their convenient distance from London proper in terms of space for abundant stabling and local supplies of fodder. The Swan stood on the site of what is now Knightsbridge Underground station. It was mentioned as early as 1636, is specifically referred to in Otway's *Soldiers of Fortune* (1681) and was rebuilt in 1777. Its innkeepers were reputedly long suspected of complicity with local highwaymen. On the opposite side of the Brompton Road stood the Marquis of Granby, the King's Head and the Rose and Crown. This last was the largest and oldest, possibly dating back to the sixteenth century. It was sufficiently celebrated to have been painted by Corbould in 1849 but was gutted by fire in 1853 and converted to a coffee-house. The Hoop and Toy near the present site of South Kensington Station may date back to *c*. 1500 and was certainly a licensed house by 1760. It was completely rebuilt in 1844 and again in 1927. The Bell and Horns, which stood where Thurloe Place joins Brompton Road, on a site now covered by Empire House, certainly dated back to the 1720s; it was rebuilt in 1824-5 and again in 1855-6 before finally being demolished in 1915.

Residential development began in 1763-4, in the aftermath of the Seven Years War, when the cessation of hostilities released discharged servicemen onto the labour market and decreased the tax burden, easing finance for building speculations. Houses, grouped in terraces of varying length, but mostly short, were built piecemeal until the 1790s when the onset of the French wars depressed building activity, except for Michael Novosielski's schemes further to the west (*see p34*). A new momentum of construction began again in the 1820s with Brompton Square, which swiftly established itself as a favoured location for theatrical and literary types. By 1827-28 a local social directory could list a hundred

38. The Bell and Horns c.1853. It stood on the Brompton Road by the junction of today's Thurloe Place. Watercolour by T.H. Shepherd.

39. Extract from Joseph Salway's survey of 1811 showing the road from Hyde Park to Counters Creek. Depicted here is the north side of Knightsbridge.

'nobility, gentry and clergy', around whom there began to cluster the households of professional persons and tradesmen of probity. By 1841 the vicar of Holy Trinity, Brompton was pleased to reassure himself that "the neighbourhood increases in respectability as well as numbers".

SMITH'S CHARITY

Henry Smith of Wandsworth (1548-1628), whipped as a beggar in his youth, went on to become a wealthy salter and Alderman of the City of London but never forgot the sting of poverty. His will included many bequests for the poor throughout his native Surrey but also required the purchase of lands for specific purposes, which led to the creation of what became an irregularly-shaped estate straggling along the Fulham Road from what is now Evelyn Gardens to the Pelham and Egerton developments. Like the Onslow complex, these names all honour trustees. One patch of land, bought with £1,000, was intended to generate £60 a year to ransom "poore Captives being slaves under the Turkish pirates". Another, of like value, was to benefit those of the donor's kin and descent deemed incapable to work for their own support. Ransoming captives having gone out of style by 1772, the two bequests were merged in that year.

The earliest development of the land for building was undertaken by Michael Novosielski (1750-95) a Roman-born architect of Polish descent, who used borrowed money to put up a straggling terrace of some forty dwellings fronting onto the Brompton Road, west of Yeoman's Row. These he dubbed eponymously – Michael's Place. They were decent enough to attract the singer Elizabeth Billington (*see p. 89*) to live at No. 16 in 1792-3 and to return to No. 33 from 1804 to 1807. William Cobbett, the radical journalist, lived at No. 11 in 1820-21, at the peak of the divorce scandal involving George IV and Queen Caroline, of whom he was a warm partisan. Michael's Place was completed by the year the architect died, heavily indebted but the square he intended to build to the rear was never built, although Michael's Grove (now Egerton Terrace) was laid out at right angles to the original terrace and some ten houses later erected along its north-east side. Novosielski also built a large house for himself. Brompton Grange, at the south

40. No. 12 Michael's Place, part of Novosielski's development along the Brompton Road, west of Yeoman's Row.

end of Yeoman's Row in 1787. This was sold to John Willett Payne (1752-1803) a sailor noted for reckless gallantry in combat and reckless dissipation off duty. Unsurprisingly Payne served as major domo to the Prince of Wales. From 1830 to 1842 the celebrated tenor singer, John Braham, (*see p. 89*) lived there. Brompton Grange was then demolished to make way for the construction of Egerton Crescent, Terrace and Place, where nearly eighty dwellings were arranged on a six-acre site. Novosielski's other houses were finally knocked down in the 1880s to be replaced by houses and shops.

The Pelham and Egerton developments of the 1830s and 1840s proceeded rapidly and successfully, their character defined by specific prohibitions on their use as lunatic asylums or brothels and against the keeping of pigs or dogs, at least in the front gardens. Architecturally they were the work of George Basevi (1794-1845) a

41. Mortimer House, in Egerton Gardens, was built in 1886-8. (See p.36.)

42. *Sir Charles Freake; from Vanity Fair 31 March 1883.*

cousin of Disraeli and pupil of Sir John Soane, architect of the Bank of England. Basevi had been appointed Surveyor to the estate in 1828 and to the Alexander estate (*see p.38*) the following year. Elsewhere Basevi would also create the terraces of Belgrave Square and the Fitzwilliam Museum in Cambridge. He was killed, at the height of his powers, by a fall from the west tower of Ely Cathedral in the course of making an architectural inspection.

After Basevi's death his surveyorship was taken over by Henry Collcutt but the dominant influence became that of the builder, Charles Freake (1814-84), who was responsible for some 330 houses, 100 stables and coach-houses, two churches and six communal gardens. The son of a coal merchant who had turned building speculator in Belgravia, Freake had himself graduated quickly from carpenter to builder and by 1843 was putting up St Jude's, Turk's Row (now demolished) in Chelsea for Basevi. It was through this contact that Freake became involved in Smith's Charity developments, signing seven building agreements with the trustees over the period 1844-83. Freake's major projects were Onslow Square (1845-65), Onslow Gardens (1863-78) and Cranley Gardens (mostly 1875-80). The residents attracted by these developments proved solidly respectable, even distinguished – the novelist Thackeray, the architects Salvin and Railton, the sculptors Marochetti and Boehm (*see p. 80*). The 1871 census revealed that the households of Onslow Square included five titled heads and an average of four servants. In Onslow Gardens the average was five.

Freake lived on the spot between 1845 and 1860, at 10 Sydney Place, and then at 19, 41 and 55 Onslow Square and 19 Sumner Place. Moving to Cromwell Road, he made his home celebrated for its musical evenings and *tableaux vivants* organised for charity. A friend of Henry Cole and the Prince of Wales, Freake built at his own cost the National Training School for Music (now the Royal College of Organists (*see pp. 92-3*), for which beneficent gesture his career was crowned with a baronetcy in 1882. At his death he left a personal estate of £718,000.

The final stage of the Smith's Charity development was the building of seventy houses in Evelyn Gardens in the decade after 1886. No. 1 was taken by J.H. Clutton of the estate's own firm of managing surveyors. Charles Digby Harrod, owner of the store in Knightsbridge, chose No. 31 for his retirement. Philip Norman, editor of the *Survey of London*, lived at No. 45 from 1890 until his death in 1931.

Subsequent redevelopments have included eccentrically Tudor Mortimer House in Egerton Gardens, built in 1886-8 for E.H. Palmer, a director of the Bank of England; Egerton Place, with designs by Mervyn Macartney, editor of *The Architectural Review*; Sussex Mansions, built 1896-1900 on the site of Sussex Terrace, a row of eight Regency period houses fronting onto Old Brompton Road; and 4-28 (even) Yeoman's Row, rebuilt as studios *c.*1900. The architect Wells Coates occupied No. 18 from 1935 to 1955, creating strikingly modernistic interiors. The mansion blocks of Crompton Court, Malvern Court and Melton Court all date from the 1930s.

43. *Onslow Square c.1851.*

44. *Nos. 9-39 Yeoman's Row in 1944. Note the Victorian shop front to the left.*

THE ALEXANDER ESTATE

The Alexander estate consisted of several holdings in various parts of Kensington. In terms of the coverage of this volume relevant sections include blocks east and west of Ashburn Place and a Brompton section now covered by Alexander Square, Alexander (originally Alfred) Place and Thurloe Square. The profits from this development were recycled to public benefit a generation later when W.H. Alexander paid for the building which currently houses the National Portrait Gallery.

The building of the Brompton section began following the bankruptcy of Harrison's nursery in 1832 (*see p29*). The building agreements specified 'large handsome fanlights', 'handsome wrought-iron balconies' and a high standard of interior finishing including cornices, papered walls, Portland stone or marble fireplaces and mahogany handrails. The development proceeded rapidly and successfully. Alexander Square was built and occupied by 1836. The 1841 census showed that on the four main streets of the estate in this area fully two-thirds of the heads of household were persons of independent means. As supervising architect Basevi brought a distinctive taste to such details as the iron-studded doors of Alexander Square, derived from the Pantheon in Rome. His surveyorship was taken over by John Blore (1818-82), a resident of Michael's Place.

The area of the Alexander estate bisected by Ashburn Place was once part of a holding called Daniel's Field, cultivated in the 1770s by nurseryman Samuel Hutchins and by 1843 by his successor, market-gardener William Attwood. Development of the area – as of the Brompton section to the east – was distorted and delayed by the incursion of the railway, which involved the compulsory purchase of obtrusive plots of land for the construction of Gloucester Road (and South Kensington) station which opened in 1868. The railway did, however, not only improve access to the area but also prompted the freeholder, H.B. Alexander, to collaborate with Lord Kensington and Robert Gunter to upgrade the Cromwell Road westward of Gloucester Road to the benefit of all three.

Development of the area west and south of Gloucester Road station began from 1870. Although private gardens were conspicuous by their absence there were three generous communal gardens. One stable was provided for every two houses. Many of the houses had billiard-

45. Alexander Square c.1905.

46 & 47 Construction work at Gloucester Road Underground station. The Metropolitan Line opened as 'Brompton (Gloucester Road)' on 1 October 1868, to be joined by the District Line a few months later in 1869.

48. Decorative stables at Ashburn Mews 1882/3.

rooms at the ground-floor rear and 'ballrooms' at the first floor rear. Beside the station a few shops were built. There were no public houses but there was Bailey's Hotel (*see p. 129*). A touch of exotic *ton* was provided by the presence of the embassy of Thailand at 21 and 23 Ashburn Place from 1884 until 1964.

As on the Gunter Estate the predominant house style changed in the later 1870s from pseudo-Italianate 'white' brick and stucco to red brick in a 'Queen Anne' or Gothic style. Much of the building was to be done by John Robertson Roberts (*see p. 43*), who lived at 103 Cromwell Road in the 1880s. Many of the designs were by architect Walter Graves (1848-1909), whose work is found throughout Earl's Court and South Kensington. The polished granite columns of the houses in Harrington Gardens reveal the taste – or perhaps the commercial interest – of their builder, John Floyd Gibbs, proprietor of a stonemason's firm in Knightsbridge, responsible for supplying many of the marble fireplaces found throughout the entire district.

The *Survey of London* notes that "amidst acres of humdrum middle class housing, sprang up two small developments which represent the extreme point of late-Victorian architectural individualism" – twenty-nine dwellings, comprising 20-26 (even) and 35-45 (odd) Harrington Gardens and 1-18A Collingham Gardens, built between 1881 and 1888 by the partnership of George and Peto.

Despite having won the R.A. Gold Medal for Architecture when he was only twenty, the career of Ernest George (1839-1922) only began to take off after he went into partnership with twenty-one year old Harold Peto (1854-1933). Harold

49. The spectacular Harrington Gardens development, designed by Ernest George & Harold Peto.

Peto's outgoing personality and business acumen were the perfect foil for George's technical brilliance and superb draughtsmanship. Peto was a son of railway contractor and Liberal MP Sir Morton Peto, whose social and business contacts were to prove invaluable to the young partners as they specialised in building for people too rich to be bothered about the cost. In the countryside this meant what a previous age would have called 'prodigy houses' and on the Alexander estate palazzi in a fantasy version of Flemish Gothic. Peto himself lived at 9 Collingham Gardens from 1885 to 1889 and then at No. 7 until 1892 when he retired from the partnership to live in the country. The thriving and fashionable practice built up by George and Peto attracted such outstanding pupils as Lutyens, Baker and Joass. George went on to be honoured with a knighthood and the presidency of the Royal Institute of British Architects. He died at his home in Kensington and was cremated at Golders Green in the crematorium which he had himself designed.

THE DAY ESTATE

The Day estate is a compact rectangle, consisting now of Wetherby Place, Rosary Gardens, Brechin Place, Hereford Square, plus an overspill now covered by the northern end of Drayton Gardens. By the 1830s residences known as Brompton Villa, Clareville, Hereford Lodge and The Rosary were ranged along the Old Brompton Road end of this estate (*see p. 24*), with a farm yard, pleasure ground, paddocks and gardens to their north. Hereford Square was begun in 1845 by James Day, whose family had owned the estate for a century. The builder was Thomas Holmes, who, though only in his twenties, had already built parts of Thurloe Square, Place and Street, and the architect was John Blore. Only the north range of nine houses has survived intact, although Pevsner notes that the architect's "supremely classical style is best witnessed on the west side, where the nine bay centrepiece with giant Corinthian paired columns and pilasters attempts to rival the best of Nash's Regent Street." Holmes was crushed by bankruptcy in 1847, so completion was delayed until 1854, instead of 1849 as projected. By 1871 half the inhabitants of Hereford Square were either retired or annuitants. Two of the houses were prep schools for boys, but of an acceptably genteel class. Noted inhabitants were to include the writer George Borrow and legendary actress Fanny Kemble.

The Drayton Gardens section of the estate was projected as early as 1845, with the intention of building 57 houses over a seven year period. In

50. Drayton Gardens c.1905.

fact it took until 1863 to cover the three-acre market garden formerly known as Rosehall. Originally known as Drayton Grove and Thistle Grove, the street was re-named in 1884 and re-numbered in 1894. The Drayton Arms was rebuilt, with an exuberant terra-cotta facade of Jacobethan grotesques, in 1891-2. To maintain the tone of the neighbourhood residents were banned from conducting any business on their premises except that of "surgeon, apothecary, sculptor, artist or seminary for young ladies."

Development of the area around Hereford Square did not begin until six years after James Day's death in 1875 but was completed by 1885. Beatrix Potter (*see p. 119*) noted in her diary in June 1883 that the rooks must have sensed something afoot as they vacated their nests in the trees felled to make way for the 88 new houses and two blocks of flats well before the cutting began. The houses built by Mineard (*see p. 52*) in Brechin Place boasted of having hot and cold water laid on from top to bottom. Sale particulars for No. 17 show it to have had a "noble dining room" with panelled ceiling and "Japanese embossed dado", eight bedrooms, a billiard-room and library, butler's pantry and separate cellars for wine and coal and no less than five lavatories. Notable inhabitants of this peripheral development included actor-manager Beerbohm Tree who lived at 31 Rosary Gardens from 1886 until 1888 and Thackeray's eldest daughter, who had a speaking-tube installed to connect the drawing-room to the nursery at 5 Wetherby Place.

51. James Gunter II.

THE GUNTER ESTATE

This estate, bounded north by Cromwell Road and south by Old Brompton Road and on the west and east by irregular boundaries between the Earl's Court Road and Ashburn Place, was laid out between *c.*1865 and *c.*1896. The land was acquired piecemeal between 1797 and 1857 by Berkeley Square confectioner James Gunter (died 1819) and his descendants. Apart from building half a dozen modest villas along the line of Old Brompton Road around 1810 for renting out, the Gunters initially concentrated on using the land as a highly profitable market-gardening business, complete with steam-heated greenhouses. By the time of James Gunter II and Robert Gunter II, however, land values had risen so much that neither had an interest in keeping on with the business and the family home at Earl's Court

52. A sale notice of 1917 of properties owned by Sir Nevill Gunter.

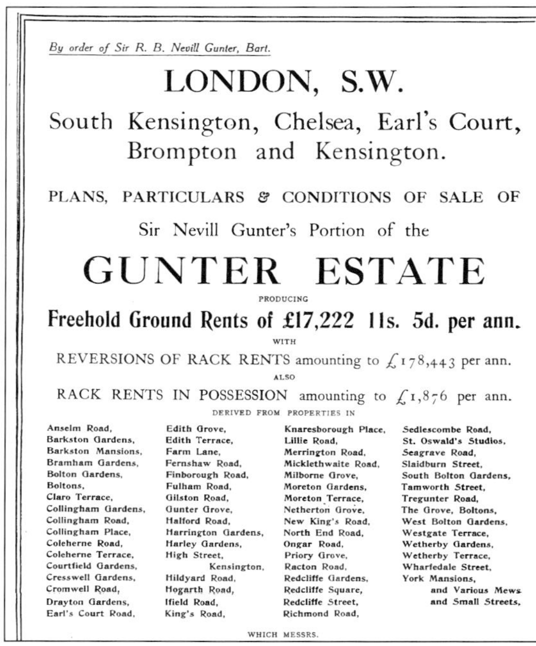

By order of Sir R. B. Nevill Gunter, Bart.

LONDON, S.W.

South Kensington, Chelsea, Earl's Court, Brompton and Kensington.

PLANS, PARTICULARS & CONDITIONS OF SALE OF

Sir Nevill Gunter's Portion of the

GUNTER ESTATE

PRODUCING

Freehold Ground Rents of £17,222 11s. 5d. per ann.

WITH

REVERSIONS OF RACK RENTS amounting to £178,443 per ann.

ALSO

RACK RENTS IN POSSESSION amounting to £1,876 per ann.

DERIVED FROM PROPERTIES IN

Anselm Road,	Edith Grove,	Knaresborough Place,	Sedlescombe Road,
Barkston Gardens,	Edith Terrace,	Lillie Road,	St. Oswald's Studios,
Barkston Mansions,	Farm Lane,	Merrington Road,	Seagrave Road,
Bramham Gardens,	Fernshaw Road,	Micklethwaite Road,	Slaidburn Street,
Bolton Gardens,	Finborough Road,	Milborne Grove,	South Bolton Gardens,
Boltons,	Fulham Road,	Moreton Gardens,	Tamworth Street,
Claro Terrace,	Gilston Road,	Moreton Terrace,	Tregunter Road,
Collingham Gardens,	Gunter Grove,	Netherton Grove,	The Grove, Boltons,
Collingham Road,	Halford Road,	New King's Road,	West Bolton Gardens,
Collingham Place,	Harrington Gardens,	North End Road,	Westgate Terrace,
Coleherne Road,	Harley Gardens,	Ongar Road,	Wetherby Gardens,
Coleherne Terrace,	High Street,	Priory Grove,	Wetherby Terrace,
Courtfield Gardens,	Kensington,	Racton Road,	Wharfedale Street,
Cresswell Gardens,	Hildyard Road,	Redcliffe Gardens,	York Mansions,
Cromwell Road,	Hogarth Road,	Redcliffe Square,	and Various Mews
Drayton Gardens,	Ifield Road,	Redcliffe Street,	and Small Streets,
Earl's Court Road,	King's Road,	Richmond Road,	

WHICH MESSRS.

53. Redcliffe Square, c.1905.

Lodge. James II was a professional soldier. Robert II decamped to Yorkshire and a political career around 1857 – hence the street names Wetherby and Knaresborough. The sixty acres developed between the mid-1860s and mid-1890s were to contain over four hundred houses (almost all in terraces), more than a hundred stables or coach-houses, a dozen blocks of flats and a church, St Jude's– but only one pub, the Clarence, at 148 Old Brompton Road. More than a score of builders were engaged in the project as lessees, including Van Camp, builder of Trebovir Road, John Robinson Roberts (1840-98), builder of Barkston Gardens and much of Harrington Gardens and George and Peto. The surveyors were George and Henry Godwin *(see p. 78).* Some of the houses put up were very large indeed. Nos. 10 and 11 Wetherby Gardens rose through five full storeys. One of Roberts's Barkston Gardens dwellings had a double drawing-room, library, conservatory, smoking-lounge, billiard-room and ten bedrooms – but only one bath-room. His flats in Barkston Gardens boasted an 'American elevator' and had from three to five reception rooms and from five to eight bed-rooms. Robertson himself died in Barkston Mansions, having recently become proprietor of the Barkston Gardens Hotel (converted from three of his houses) and worth over £100,000. Such properties were often slow to let and many waited up to four years between completion and occupation. Eminent inhabitants of the estate area were to include sculptor Sir J.E. Boehm (*see p. 80*) and, a generation later, retired Field Marshal Allenby (*see p. 112*). The high standing of the inhabitants is indicated by the presence not of mere servants but of several butlers. Although there was no general descent to the boarding-house level, as happened further west, conversion of unmanageably large properties into apartments had begun even before the outbreak of the Great War. By the 1920s mews stables were being turned into 'bijou' cottages.

The Boltons and Redcliffe Square section of the Gunter estate, amounting to some 93 acres, was still open land in 1800, used as market gardens and orchards and a source of brick earth and gravel. As architect George Godwin reminisced in 1875, "We remember an old friend who used to say the adjacent field [Thistle Grove] was never without a hare and that he had out of the window counted six brace of partridge rise from the Boltons." The area was subsequently covered with 1,100 houses, plus two churches and five public houses. Development began from 1850 onwards, starting in Gilston Road and Tregunter Road and ending with the completion of Redcliffe Square in 1876. The east side of The Boltons was erected in 1851-2, the west in 1857-60. Early occupants included artist Charles Vacher, S. Carter Hall, the editor of the *Art Journal*, civil engineer Sir Robert Rawlinson and Benjamin Golding, founder of the Charing Cross Hospital. Subsequent residents included W.S. Gilbert and dramatist Brandon Thomas. Bousfield Primary School was built on the bombed-out site of Beatrix Potter's former home in 1954-6.

BROMPTON HOSPITAL ESTATE

The Brompton Hospital Estate consists of Neville Terrace, Neville Street and Foulis Terrace.

The hospital was the first to be specifically designated for the treatment of tuberculosis, a disease which pre-existing institutions had shunned as untreatable. It was the brain-child of solicitor Philip Rose, a friend of Disraeli. Rose was ultimately rewarded with a baronetcy in 1874, the year in which Disraeli became Prime Minister for the second time.

The hospital site itself, formerly part of the nursery of William Malcolm, was bought from the Smith's Charity estate, the rest from the fifth Earl of Harrington. In the seventeenth century this part had been Richard Selwood's nursery, then Rubergall's, famed for its lettuces, then Curtis's Botanic Garden (*see p. 31*). H-shaped for maximum ventilation, the Tudor-style hospital building was designed by F.J.Francis. The foundation stone was laid by the Prince Consort in 1844 and the first patients were admitted in 1846, although the building was not completed until 1854, St. Luke's chapel having been added in 1849-50. In its design the hospital paid careful attention to heating and ventilation, having small wards and wide corridors. Steam-power was ingeniously exploited, not only to heat the building and the water-supply but even to operate lifts, turn the kitchen spit and grind coffee. When the National Health Service was established in 1948 the Brompton Hospital became the designated centre of expertise for teaching about chest diseases. The original building was converted to apartments in 1999-2000.

54. Brompton Hospital, designed by F.J. Francis, was opened in 1846.

LITTLE CHELSEA

Running along the Fulham Road from Thistle Grove to Redcliffe Gardens, Little Chelsea's southern boundary is neatly defined by the road itself, its northern boundary by contrast a ragged line of varying depth from the highway. Fragmented in ownership and development, it evolved as a mixed community of villas, cottages, businesses, public houses and private madhouses. Built and re-built over more than two centuries, Seymour Walk remains as a dignified and tranquil late Georgian survival. Lochee's military academy (*see p. 67*) was one of its most distinctive features.

THE WARE ESTATE

The Ware estate, consisting of Elm Place, Elm Mews, Selwood Terrace and Selwood Place, was built on the market garden owned by Francis Shailer between 1802 and 1823. The land was bought by Samuel Ware, architect of the Burlington Arcade, when Shailer's twenty-one year lease ran out. Building was completed between 1824 and 1836. In 1835 Dickens lodged briefly at 11 Selwood Terrace to be near his fiancée. D.H. Lawrence stayed briefly at No. 9 in 1914.

THE BILLINGS

The name of the Billings recalls 'Billingwell Dyche', which became Counter's (possibly from Countess) Creek, which forms the western boundary of this tiny enclave. The Creek, converted in 1824-8 to become the Kensington Canal, was converted again in 1859-63 to become a section of the West London Extension Railway. The Billings estate was built between 1844 and 1856. The census of 1861 shows its occupants to have been entirely working-class, the most part employed as building tradesmen, transport workers, gardeners and laundresses. Average occupancy was high at 8.3 per house, with eighteen crammed into 1 Billing Street. Social transformation dates from the 1950s when Douglas Fairbanks's daughter moved in.

Proximity to Chelsea football ground has doubtless proved a double-edged attraction.

55. The residence of M. La Touche of Little Chelsea, now the site of Seymour Place.

56. Selwood Place, north side in June 1937.

57. Billing's Well, usually called Counter's Creek, was later converted into the Kensington Canal and was later built over by the West London Extension Railway.

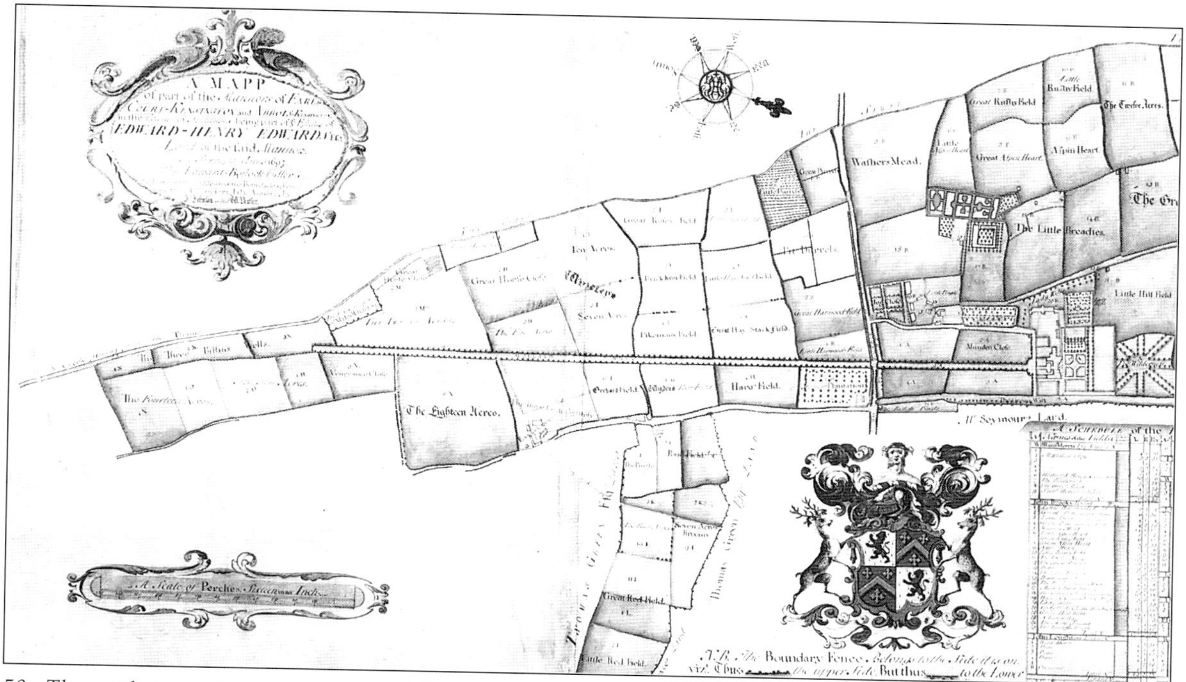

58. *The southern portion of the estate of Edward, Earl of Warwick and Holland, taken from a 1734 copy of a Survey by Edward Fuller 1694-95.*

Earl's Court

THE EDWARDES ESTATE

The largest estate in Kensington in the early nineteenth century, some 250 acres in extent, belonged to William Edwardes (1712-1801) MP and first Baron Kensington (a title in the Irish peerage). The Edwardes family's home county was Pembrokeshire in west Wales, where they held considerable landed property – hence such local street names as Pembroke, Philbeach, Longridge, Nevern and Penywern. Edwardes was a descendant of Sir Walter Cope, who had purchased the manor of Kensington in c.1604 from a descendant of the Aubrey de Vere who really did come over with the Conqueror. The estate, once the home farm of the lords of the manor, consisted of a wedge of fields, running north-south, from the line of what is now High Street Kensington, narrowing in its bottom third, south of Old Brompton Road (mostly now covered by Brompton Cemetery), with a spur jutting out to the east in what is now the area of Lexham Gardens.

When William Edwardes (1777-1852) second Baron Kensington succeeded in 1801 aged 24, Earl's Court Farm accounted for some 190 acres of the estate. Tenanted by generations of the Hutchins family, it was used for mixed arable farming and market gardening. The farmhouse, roughly on the site of Earl's Court station, was occupied by the farm bailiff. Samuel Hutchins, the tenant, lived in a detached newly-built brick Manor House (*ill. 60*) just to the north. Both buildings were demolished in 1875-8 to make way for houses either side of the new Metropolitan District Railway station, constructed in 1865-9 in a cutting squeezed in between them.

The second Baron increased his income from the estate by renewing short-term leases at higher rents but valued it chiefly as a security against which to borrow some £20,000, having accumulated debts of some £10,000 before even succeeding to his inheritance. By 1828 Kensington's debts had more than doubled again to £55,000. Attempts to develop the land through speculators proved ill-fated. Edwardes Square took some fifteen years to complete. The canal constructed along Counter's Creek, which defined the western boundary of the estate and the parish, was opened with bravura celebrations in 1828 but failed commercially. Following London's second outbreak of cholera in 1848-9 it was filled

59. (Above) Earl's Court Farm in the 1860s. Samuel Alloway is in the left-hand cart.

60. (Left) Earl's Court Manor House in c.1845.

in as a health hazard. Substantial schemes in the Warwick Gardens and Pembroke Square areas were aborted by bankruptcies following a national financial crisis in 1825. By 1833 the second baron was on the brink of total insolvency but managed to entail the Kensington estate to his heir, another William, on the eve of his marriage. The rest of the second Baron's life continued as a maelstrom of debt-juggling and ultimately fruitless land-dealing which reduced him to a household consisting of one male servant and an illegitimate daughter. His will characterised his legacy as 'embarrassed and in great confusion' – a masterpiece of legal understatement, given that he was worth less than £100 and had debts of £270,000.

By 1860, however, the third baron had secured his right to undisputed possession of the Kensington lands entailed for his benefit. Between 1862 and 1867 he received £100,000 from railway companies for some 30 acres of this land, enabling him to pay off outstanding mortgages of £66,000. The construction of the Metropolitan

District Railway from 1865 onwards transformed Earl's Court from farmland to a densely-populated suburb of 1,200 houses and two churches in the quarter century after 1867.

A renewed entail ensured the succession of the estate to the fourth Lord Kensington in 1872. Like the first baron he represented Haverfordwest as MP for some years and in 1886 was created Baron Kensington in the English peerage. His sudden death in 1896 left the fifth / second baron, a 28-year-old bachelor, with an annual rental income of £20,000. In 1900 he died of wounds in the Boer war. The estate passed to his brother, who by 1905 had sold it off to reinvest the proceeds in financial assets. Large tracts were owned for some years by Lord Iveagh of the Guinness brewing dynasty and Sir John Ellerman, the shipping magnate, before passing into the portfolios of major financial institutions and then fragmenting into a complex pattern of ownership during the volatile property market fluctuations of the 1970s.

The part of the Edwardes estate to the south of West Cromwell Road, which falls within the area covered by this book, was developed almost entirely after the advent of the Metropolitan District Railway.

The fan-shaped area of Eardley Crescent and Kempsford Gardens radiates out from a corner pub, erected in 1864 as the Lord Ranelagh. Built as a single speculation between 1867 and 1873, it packed 160 houses and a group of stables into just six acres. In 1887-8, No.58 Eardley Crescent was briefly occupied by the Irish painter John Butler Yeats and his two talented sons, Jack B., the future painter and William Butler, the future poet and Nobel Laureate. Lily Yeats thought the house "horrible" and dismissed its 'garden' as "a bit of cat-haunted sooty gravel". The Yeats household soon moved on with gratitude to the artsy new garden suburb of Bedford Park.

The streets of this compact sub-estate rapidly acquired a distinctive social ranking. Eardley Crescent in 1881 boasted a Colonel and a Rear-Admiral, each with three servants, while, of the 38 houses in Kempsford Gardens, only nine had servants, twenty-four were in multiple occupation and two were lodging-houses. Of the fifteen 'householders' of Kramer Mews no less than nine were common cabmen.

61. A railway crash at Earl's Court station in August 1885.

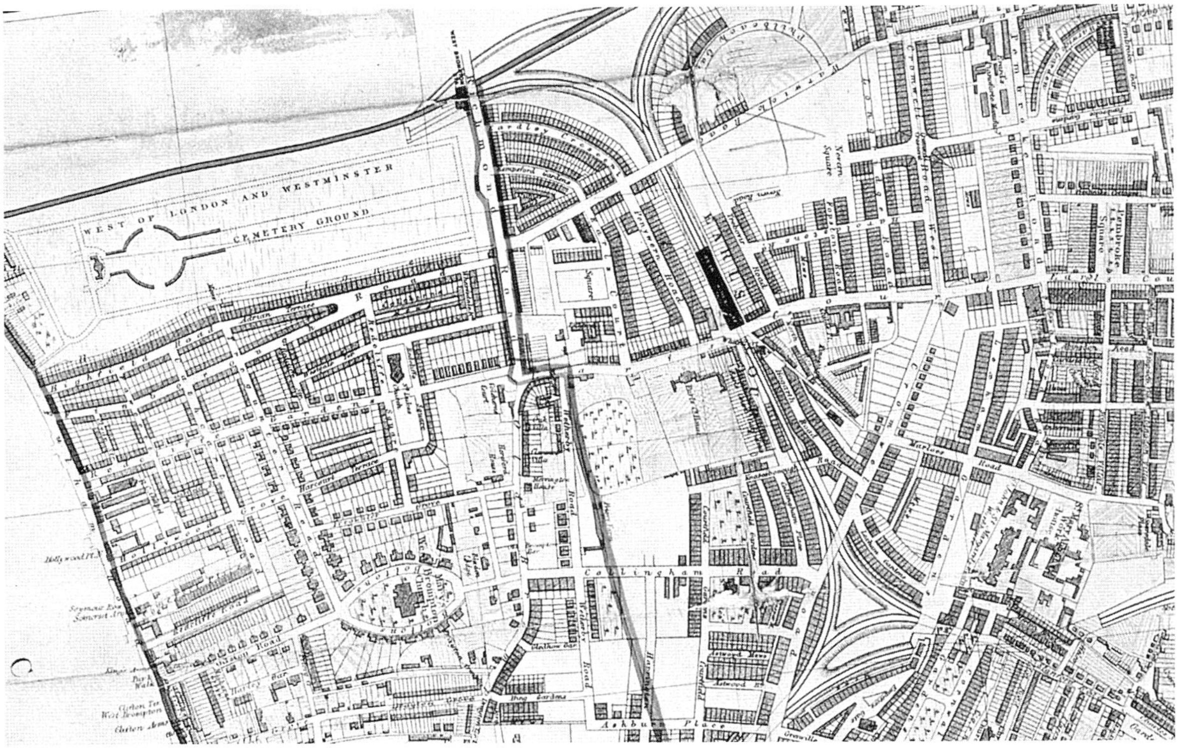

62. Daws map of 1879 showing development around Philbeach Gardens (centre top) with Nevern Square marked but not built just below it. The area between Philbeach Gardens and Eardley Crescent is now covered by the Earl's Court Exhibition Centre. North is to the right.

63. Kempsford Gardens, c.1905.

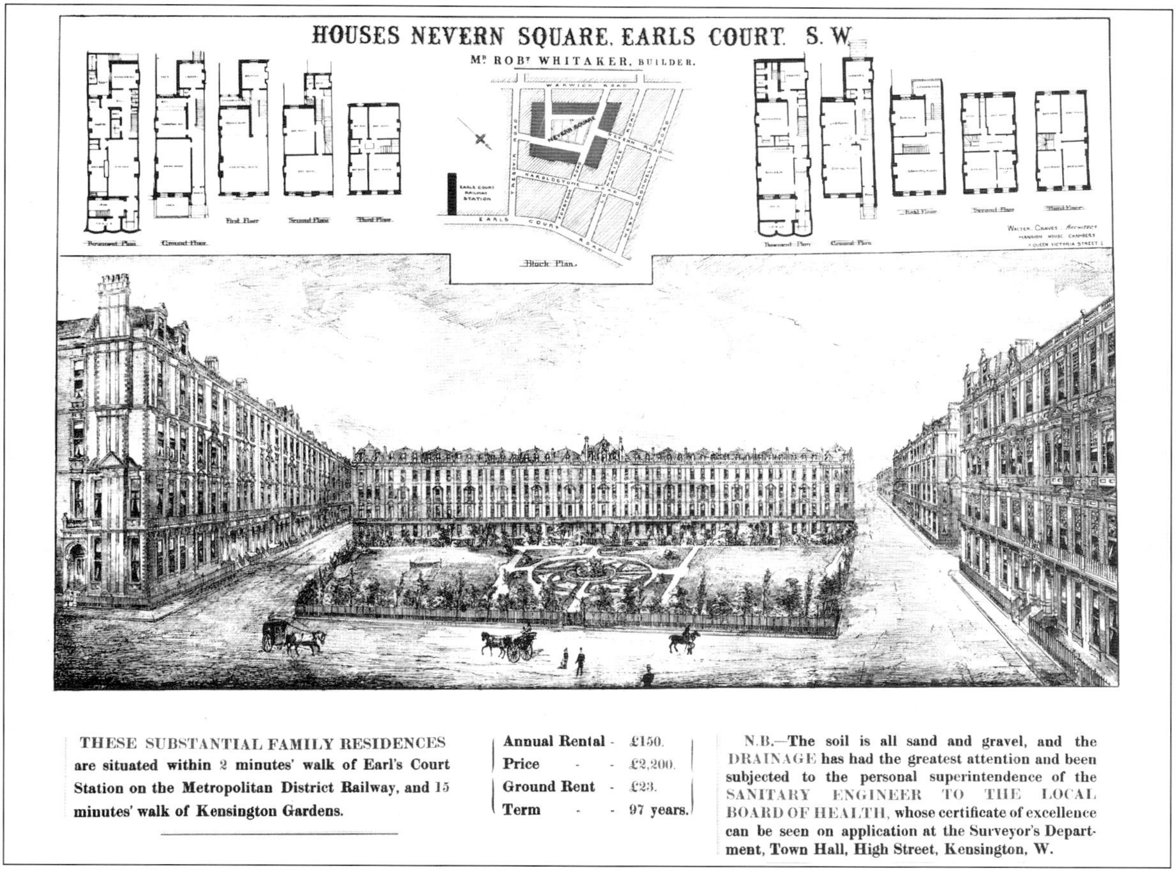

64. Advertisement for houses in Nevern Square in c.1880. The price of a house was £2,200 or an annual rental of £150.

Building began in Earl's Court Square and Longridge Road in 1873, in Nevern Place in 1874, in Trebovir Road and Philbeach Gardens in 1876 and Nevern Square in 1880. By the 1890s the few remaining vacant plots were being filled with mansion blocks. The area attracted highly respectable residents – assuming one was willing to overlook the private life of Ellen Terry. Her neighbours in Longridge Road in 1881 included novelist Marie Corelli, a convivial spirit in the shape of the business manager of the Haymarket Theatre and possibly less convivial ones in the shape of half a dozen barristers and ten widows living off investments. Not one home in the street was without servants, most had three, some four.

Two homes in Longridge Road were, however, already sub-divided and two more had become boarding-houses. In Trebovir Road several of the larger houses (built 1876-9) were to become hotels. Contemporaries viewed this development askance. Charles Booth, doyen of social investigators who lived at 6 Grenville Place, observed with cold irony that "the tide of fashion and favour which for some time flowed towards Brompton exhausted itself in the Wild West of Earl's Court". His painstaking surveys of the distribution of poverty throughout the metropolis revealed how deceptive superficial appearances could be. In many streets classified as merely 'well-to-do' the houses, although they might contain few servants, remained real homes, occupied by the same families continuously. Other streets, however, with perhaps apparently grander houses, which may but recently have merited the designation 'wealthy', were no longer what they seemed: "Houses are now occupied, now empty; tenants come and go. The house, a home no longer, is made a source of income. There are guests who pay, or the drawing-room floor is let, or boarders are taken, or at length

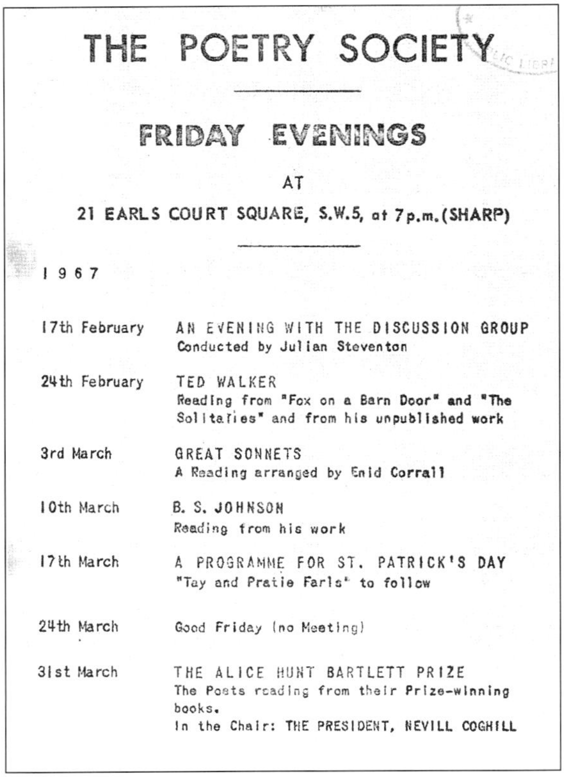

THE POETRY SOCIETY

FRIDAY EVENINGS

AT

21 EARLS COURT SQUARE, S.W.5, at 7p.m.(SHARP)

1967

17th February	AN EVENING WITH THE DISCUSSION GROUP Conducted by Julian Steventon
24th February	TED WALKER Reading from "Fox on a Barn Door" and "The Solitaries" and from his unpublished work
3rd March	GREAT SONNETS A Reading arranged by Enid Corrall
10th March	B. S. JOHNSON Reading from his work
17th March	A PROGRAMME FOR ST. PATRICK'S DAY "Tay and Pratie Farls" to follow
24th March	Good Friday (no Meeting)
31st March	THE ALICE HUNT BARTLETT PRIZE The Poets reading from their Prize-winning books. In the Chair: THE PRESIDENT, NEVILL COGHILL

65. Some social life in Earl's Court in 1967. The Poetry Society met at 21 Earl's Court Square.

the fatal word 'Apartments' appears in the fan-light over the door. Against its downfall each street struggles in vain. Those who can afford to do so leave the stricken district ...".

Apart from sub-division into apartments or conversion into hotels, a few large houses were destined for other fates. In 1913 Nos. 254-6 and 258-60 Earl's Court Road were joined together as premises for the Brompton and Knightsbridge Electric Supply Company with offices, a show-room and an oak-panelled restaurant intended to demonstrate the advantages of cooking with electricity.

The Philbeach Gardens area was the work of George Edward Mineard, born in Newfound-land in 1838, who also built Lexham Gardens. Mineard sought the advice of Sir Henry Cole (*see p. 104*) on such matters as tree-planting and electric lighting: it was as well he did, as the advice would probably have been proffered anyway. No. 96, Cole's old house, was recon-structed in 1947 after war damage.

Nevern Square, according to estate surveyor Daniel Cubitt Nichols, was "occupied princi-pally by a large number of retired army men and they are not very easy to satisfy as a rule." The author Compton Mackenzie (1883-1972) and his sister, actress Fay Compton (1894-1978) lived at

66. The proposed Philbeach Gardens development pictured in the builder's prospectus, a prospect only partly realised.

No. 1 Nevern Square, bought by their father in 1901 for £2,000 – £1,500 less than its original sale price in 1881. Like a number of other properties in the square it had to be rebuilt after severe bomb damage in World War Two.

The first resident of No. 1 Earl's Court Square in 1874 was military inventor Sir William Palliser (1830-82) whose invention of a cheap method of converting smooth-bore cannon to rifled ordnance netted him some £15,000. In all he held more than a dozen patents and was an expert on technical subjects ranging from fortifications to fastenings. By 1877 Palliser was living at No. 19 and from 1878 until his early death at No. 21, which later became the home of the Poetry Society (*see ill. 65*). Palliser used his personal fortune to finance the building of Nos. 25-31 Earl's Court Square and the proposed development of the whole south side but did not live to enjoy the fruits of his investment, his health broken, it was claimed, by a bitter feud with War Office officialdom over a number of his patents. He still died worth £89,689. When the houses on the south side of the square were eventually built the first occupant, of No. 36 in 1896, was stockbroker Frank Gielgud, father of the actor Sir John Gielgud (1904-2000),who moved on in 1904 to 7 Gledhow Gardens, where John was born that year. Another youthful occupant of the square was the future Dame Ninette de Valois (nee Edris Stannus), who lived at No. 23 in the home of her mother at the start of her career. By 1910 there were eight boarding-houses in the square, plus two private hotels and a dancing school. Earl's Court Square was declared a Conservation Area in 1975.

67. Earl's Court Road in 1850.

68. New shops and apartments in Earl's Court Road.

EARL'S COURT VILLAGE

The tangle of streets east of Earl's Court Road, opposite the station, corresponding to ancient Pound Field, was designated a Conservation Area in 1973. Far from constituting an entity, in the sense of a single estate, it was built up piecemeal by over a dozen different developers, ranging from Lord Kensington and Robert Gunter II, to J.L. Tomlin, Gunter's solicitor, Van Camp a Belgian-born builder, Alfred Savigear, publican of the Prince of Teck and Thomas Smith, vintner of Chelsea and his nephew C.W. Wallgrave. To call this area a 'Village' is to reflect the modest size of the houses and the shops intermingled with them, rather than to imply any obvious physical nucleus, such as a church or green. By the 1680s there was a brewhouse near the present

185 Earl's Court Road and by the 1720s a tavern, the White Hart (*ill. 157*), to the west of the present No. 2 Hogarth Road. In so far as one can speak of a village this was its nucleus. By 1740 there was a forge in operation at what became 21 Kenway Road; it finally closed in 1907. An isolated terrace of four dwellings – The Terrace – stood from *c.*1760 to the 1870s on the site of 189-203 Earl's Court Road. Its early inhabitants included the Sardinian envoy, Francois, Comte de Viry and the anatomist John Hunter (*see p26*).

Nothing further was developed until Thomas Smith began building small houses on Pound Field around 1803-5 in the area of Kenway Road and Hogarth Place. By the 1830s the local population was still under a thousand. Of Smith's speculation 35-71 (odd) Kenway Road (but not including 57-61, which were rebuilt) survive from *c.*1807-10; originally known as Manor Terrace, then Earl's Court Terrace, then Providence Terrace in 1851, it was renamed and renumbered as Kenway Road in 1908. The 1851 census reveals that in the nineteen houses were twenty-four households of rather mixed but broadly petit-bourgeois standing. Eight kept a servant. Occupations of household heads ranged from an Inspector at the Great Exhibition and a stockbroker, to Treasury clerks and a parochial schoolmaster, to coachman and journeyman baker. Four houses had already been sub-divided for multiple occupation. Perhaps the downward level of the street had already been determined by the fact that after 1819 land nearby had been given over to such noisome enterprises as a brewery, a wax-bleaching works and a factory for making floor-cloth canvas. The wax-bleaching works served Samuel Childs' wax-chandler's business, off Leicester Square, until he closed the works around 1852 and began redevelopment to create Child's Street and Child's Place, where in 1861 the servantless homes had an average of seven inhabitants each in households headed variously by policemen, gardeners, piano-makers and a

69. Shops in Hogarth Place in 1904.

70. The publican and developer, Alfred Savigear, also ran a riding school beween Kenway Road and Child's Place.

71. Templeton Place c.1905.

'laundress at home'. Their rents enabled Childs himself to live as a gentleman in genteel exile out at Sunbury. Wallgrave Road and Terrace, dating from the 1860s, by when the local population had climbed to five thousand, seem to have accepted multiple occupation from the start, having an average of thirteen residents per house, including several categorised as common labourers. Hogarth Road, by contrast, built between 1873 and 1876 by solicitor J.L. Tomlin, counted among its occupants three clergymen, a major and even an admiral. James Wyld, the geographer and promoter of the Great Globe tourist attraction in Leicester Square, lived at No. 25. Tomlin was also responsible for building the north side of Earl's Court Gardens and the west end of its south side plus The Courtfield public house adjacent at 187 Earl's Court Road. The advent of the railway in 1871 hastened commercial development, with house-fronts being built out into shops in the 1870s in Earl's Court Gardens, Hogarth Place and Kenway Road. In 1880 Savigear the publican built 1-13 (odd) Kenway Road as shops with flats over. In 1886 a Turkish baths was built at 24A Earl's Court Gardens where it survived until World War Two. In 1892 Savigear diversified his interests still further to open a riding school (*see p. 70*) on a leftover patch of ground between Kenway Road and Child's Place. By the 1920s the establishment was given over to light industrial use.

Wartime bombing inflicted much random damage on this area and wartime dislocations brought it many new inhabitants, if often only briefly, in the immediate post-war era. Polish refugees were initially conspicuous. These forced migrants were followed by others voluntarily seeking wider horizons, students from former British colonies, and then, with the establishment of the Overseas Visitors Club in Templeton Place in the 1950s, South Africans, Rhodesians and Australians eager to taste London and use it as a springboard for further travels. By the 1970s the new incomers were Arabs, Iranians and Filipinos. Thanks to the Piccadilly Line and Cromwell Road links with Heathrow airport Earl's Court had become not only the gateway to London but the unwitting seismograph of globalisation and a microcosm of the multicultural society.

Albert's Memorial

ALBERT, THE MAN

Albert of Saxe-Coburg-Gotha (1819-61) epitomised the classic Victorian values of duty, diligence and faith in progress. A minor German princeling, he was chosen to marry his cousin, Victoria, in 1840, three years after she became Queen of England. Albert was an idealist of energy and vision, but compelled by his constitutional position to walk in the shadow of his wife. As a foreigner and an intellectual he was suspect to the social and political elites of his adopted country and he fulfilled many of their worst fears by effectively becoming the Queen's most trusted adviser. She adored and idealised him, recognising that he was not only cleverer than she was but also less impetuous and more methodical. Their love was grounded in a physical relationship which swiftly produced nine children. Their other shared passions included Scotland, German music and practical jokes. Albert eliminated much waste and inefficiency in the royal household, improved agriculture on the royal farms and reorganised the chaotic royal art collection. His other interests embraced the decoration of the new Houses of Parliament and the reform of housing, the army and the University of Cambridge. He designed royal homes at Osborne and Balmoral and together with Victoria took piano lessons from Mendelssohn and etching lessons from Landseer.

Albert's biggest project, the Great Exhibition of 1851 was a triumphant success, despite all predictions to the contrary. The Prince Consort surrounded himself with able, cultured men whose names are a roll-call of Victorian enterprise – the builder Thomas Cubitt, who helped him build the royal summer residence at Osborne, Joseph Paxton, designer of the Crystal Palace, Henry Cole, first Director of the Victoria & Albert Museum and Sir Charles Eastlake, first Director of the National Gallery. Almost the last thing Albert did was fend off an Anglo-American war. Dying suddenly of typhoid at 42, Albert had indeed lived "a life dedicated to the public good" as his memorial subsequently proclaimed. British guilt about the rather shabby way he had been treated compensated by attaching his name to streets, pubs and public institutions throughout the land. Victoria mourned him obsessively until her own death forty years later.

72. Prince Albert, from the painting by F. Winterhalter.

THE MEMORIAL

The Memorial, magnificently restored in a multi-million pound refurbishment completed in 1999, was regarded as so appalling in the 1950s that its total demolition was seriously discussed. It is now recognised as an icon of Victorian taste, technology and ideology.

Public donations to a fund started by the Lord Mayor of London in 1862 raised £60,000, topped up by £50,000 voted in Parliament. The competition for the design was won by Sir George Gilbert Scott (1811-1878) who had the largest architectural practice in the country and whose other major London works include the Foreign Office and St Pancras Station hotel. Scott's inspirations for the memorial design include German medieval reliquaries, the monument to Sir Walter Scott in Edinburgh and the 'Eleanor Crosses' originally erected by Edward I, like the one outside Charing Cross station which was rebuilt in medieval style in 1865. The completed memorial incorporates much hidden hi-tech, standing as it does on an artificial mound of 868

73. The Albert Memorial in the 1870s.

brick arches, supported on massive layers of masonry, which in turn rest on a raft of concrete 16 feet thick. The spire is of iron, supported by a concealed cruciform iron box-girder. Work was finally completed in 1876 and earned Scott his knighthood.

The Albert Memorial is more than a nation's tribute to a man; it is also a nation's tribute to itself, expressed in a complex iconography which represents a Victorian view of culture, civilisation, technology and the world order. Four complementary sculpture groups symbolize nations contributing to the Great Exhibition of 1851. America has a theme – Advance ! The USA, with a band of stars on her dress, points the way forward. Canada holds a rose, symbol of England, to her breast. When this group was designed America had just come through a terrible civil war and was re-asserting its customary self-confidence. It was therefore thought undiplomatic to make Canada the dominant figure. Mexico had just thrown out the armies of French emperor Napoleon III, hence its representation as an athletic Aztec warrior. The rest of South America is subsumed into a somnolent gaucho.

In Greek myth Europa is carried to Zeus by a bull. The central figure of the European group has an orb and sceptre, symbolizing European rule over the world. Britain carries a trident – for sea-power – and a shield with the crosses of St George and St Andrew. France's sword stands for martial glory, Germany's book for art and science. Italy, recently united, awakens from lost centuries; a lyre and palette acknowledging her excellence in music and painting. Asia shows a Persian holding a pen, perhaps a reference to Edward Fitzgerald's 1859 translation of the *Rubaiyat of Omar Khayyam*. A Chinese makes porcelain, a familiar export representing China's achievements in both art and technology. The Arab has his Qur'an. India is a warrior, perhaps a memory of the suppression of the rebellion of 1857-8 against British rule. The African group focuses on North Africa, as little was then known of the continent's interior. Originally a lion was to be used as the focus but this was dropped in favour of a camel, to avoid confusion with the British Lion. The Egyptian princess represents Africa's greatest past civilization. Near the Nubian a half-buried statue represents other lost ancient cultures. There is also an Arab trader and an African whose broken shackles commemo-

74. Fashions in Hyde Park – on the steps of the Albert Memorial – in July 1873.

rate Britain's abolition of slavery within its empire in 1834. The African listens attentively to a European figure, representing advanced civilisation.

The Parnassus Frieze runs around the podium below the statue of Albert himself, carrying 169 figures. The poets and musicians, predominantly German, and painters, mostly Italian, run chronologically. The sculptors and architects also run chronologically. The only living person was G.G. Scott himself, included at Victoria's personal insistence and shown in profile looking at his master, Pugin. Michelangelo is included twice, as are references to Florence and the Parthenon. The large number of medieval characters reflects both Scott's own preferences and Victorian interest in the Middle Ages. Nowadays it looks extraordinary to rank Wilkie alongside Turner or to include such figures as Bishop, Auber and Thorwaldsen with Dante or Raphael.

The statuary represents Industrial Arts – Agriculture (the retort and cylinder denote the scientific application of chemistry and steam-power), Manufactures (Britain's staple industries – Iron, Textiles and Pottery, plus a beehive for industriousness and an hour-glass for Time), Commerce (a cornucopia plus scales and a ledger; the bag of corn representing Necessities, the casket, Luxuries), Engineering (a navvy, plus steam-hammer and blast-furnace and Robert Stephenson's Menai and Britannia bridges). Other groups show the Greater Sciences – Geometry, Astronomy, Chemistry, Geology, Physiology, Rhetoric, Medicine, Philosophy; the Christian Virtues – Faith, Hope, Fortitude, Prudence, Justice, Temperance. The mosaics show four arts, each including two of its greatest practitioners – Poetry (Homer and King David), Painting (Apelles and Raphael), Architecture (Solomon and Ictinus) and Sculpture (Phidias and Michelangelo).The statue of Albert was cast of bronze from captured enemy cannon. Albert is shown holding a thick book, marking a place with his finger – not the Bible, but the catalogue of the exhibits of the Great Exhibition.

Albertopolis

THE ROYAL HORTICULTURAL SOCIETY

For a quarter of a century most of what is now the site of Imperial College and the Science Museum was occupied by the gardens of the Royal Horticultural Society. This not entirely suitable location arose out of a perceived coincidence of wants and an actual coincidence of patronage. Prince Albert was both the recently-elected President of the R.H.S. and also President of the 1851 Exhibition Commissioners. The R.H.S. was going through a period of difficulties. Albert believed that a spectacular new garden in the midst of his emerging cultural complex would both give the R.H.S. a much-needed boost and provide a pleasing focus for the still raw structures going up all around the area, as well as enhancing the potential residential value of the Commissioners' as yet undeveloped property. The actual design of the gardens was technically assigned to Henry Cole, Francis Fowke and Richard Redgrave of the Science and Art department, with architect Sydney Smirke as consultant; but the Prince Consort himself took the closest possible personal interest in planning the details of the Italianate garden, to the point of choosing the colour of the bricks used for its walls and even advising on the best manufacturer for them. Albert also helped materially with funding the project by mobilising his fellow royals to make donations and assisting the Society to style itself 'Royal'. These initiatives marked the cause as worthy of the support of the fashionable world and ensured the rapid accumulation of the £50,000 needed for the Society to match the £50,000 put up by the Commissioners for the basic landscaping. Victoria found Albert's virtual obsession with the project 'tiresome', a sentiment she may thereafter have regretted as he died within less than a year of its opening.

The gardens, twenty acres of terraces and arcades, shrubbery and statuary, were bisected by canals and coloured gravel paths and punctuated by two elegant bandstands and large trees which were already growing on the site, the whole assemblage being overshadowed by an immense (265′ x 96′ x 75′) gas-lit conservatory

75. A view of the Royal Horticultural Society's Gardens from the International Exhibition Hall in 1862.

of iron and glass. The result was an instant London landmark. Capitalising on the gardens' centrality and accessibility, the R.H.S. used them to promote flower shows which not only spread an appreciation of new varieties but also, by awarding prizes, encouraged the novel art of flower-arranging. In the long run, however, the enterprise was doomed. The R.H.S. continued to suffer financial problems and there was friction with local residents and with a faction of R.H.S. members who considered the gardens too much given over to amusements such as bands and bowls and too little to scientific horticulture. Above all there was the inexorable problem of central London's fog, which by the 1870s was reaching a new peak of smoke-enriched foulness. By the 1880s the R.H.S. gardens were no more remarkable than any averagely well-kept municipal park. In 1883 the grounds were given over to an International Fisheries Exhibition, in 1884 to an International Health Exhibition. The theme of health was very broadly interpreted to embrace a Japanese restaurant and a reconstruction of an 'Old London' street, complete with the alleged houses of Izaak Walton and Dick Whittington. The Society bowed out at last rather ignominiously in 1888 and by 1892 new roads and buildings had obliterated much of the former site, though some of the original arcades, cannibalised to serve adjacent institutions as classrooms or store-rooms, survived as late as the 1950s.

THE INTERNATIONAL EXHIBITION OF 1862

The huge success of the 'Great Exhibition' of 1851 confounded the Jeremiahs who had predicted not only massive financial losses but a crime wave, major riots and an epidemic. But a proposal to repeat the enterprise a decade later was greeted with little enthusiasm by Prince Albert, who thought it unlikely that a repeat performance could be anything like as successful as the original venture. Henry Cole, however, was a difficult man to dissuade. Even a war involving France, Austria and Italy – three major potential participants – only caused him to delay, not shelve, his plans. The untimely death of the Prince Consort in 1861 removed another negative influence and the exhibition finally went ahead in 1862. The design of the exhibition building was entrusted to Cole's protégé, Francis Fowke. What he produced turned out to be both wider and higher than the Crystal Palace but not nearly as elegant. Even the guidebook produced by Messrs. Chambers conceded that "the structure, as a whole, does not profess to be in any particular style; professional architects say little in its praise; nor is the public favourably impressed ... ". Located along the newly-constructed Cromwell Road, to the south side of the Royal Horticultural Society's barely-finished grounds, Fowke's monster consisted of a vaulted nave flanked to two domed transepts, each dome being broader and taller than those of either the Pantheon in Rome or of the Reading Room of the British Museum. Covering some twenty-five acres, the exhibition building incorporated some seven million bricks and it was widely assumed that the Cromwell Road frontage "will unquestionably be permanent".

The organizing principles of 1862 differed significantly from those of 1851. Fine arts were to be included as well as industry. The latter should include only items produced since 1851 and should attempt wherever possible to demonstrate processes as well as products – needle-making as well as needles, printing as well as prints. Fine art exhibits were to be modern but the definition of the notion was left to the discretion of exhibitors, many of whom stretched it up to a century. In retrospect the most significant exhibits turned out to cross the boundaries of art and industry, being the earliest furniture to be produced by William Morris's newly-founded firm of Morris, Marshall, Faulkner & Co. Despite not having a railway station nearer than two kilometres – Chambers advised taking a steamboat to Cadogan Pier or making the most of a walk through Hyde Park – the exhibition did manage to match the six million attendance figure of 1851 but registered a deficit of £11,000, which was made up by the contractor for the exhibition building, John Kelk of Pimlico. Despite predictions of its permanence, public dislike of the exhibition building was so strong that by 1864 Henry Cole was sketching its half-demolished ruins and the site was shortly after redeveloped as the new home of the Natural History Museum.

THE ROYAL ALBERT HALL

The site of the Albert Hall might have become the home of a new National Gallery but thanks to the ubiquitous Henry Cole it was developed to serve primarily as a concert hall. It was Cole who in 1864 conceived the idea of financing its construction by selling seats to private subscribers. Over 1,300 were sold at £100 each. The government endorsed the scheme in 1866 and the design was entrusted to Captain Fowke again, in preference to the far more eminent George Gilbert Scott. A major inspiration appears to have been the Dresden Opera built in 1837-41 to the designs of Gottfried Semper, another member of the Henry Cole entourage. Prince Albert had, indeed, asked Semper to draw up plans but these were not used, nor were those for Fowke's first scheme, prematurely drawn up in 1858, which aimed at a capacity of 15,000, almost twice as much as the building was eventually to accommodate. Fowke's sudden and early death meant that responsibility for completing the project passed to another military man, Maj.-Gen. H.Y.D. Scott. It was Scott who added what are perhaps the Hall's most striking external features, its projecting balcony and terracotta frieze celebrating the Triumph of Arts and Letters. The Hall's decorative mosaic panels were made up by the ladies of the South Kensington Museum mosaic class, in which Henry Cole's female relatives were prominently represented. Scott was also responsible for the dome, Fowke having envisaged a flat ceiling. The Albert Hall was opened in 1871 by the Prince of Wales, as the occasion had threatened to become too emotional for his mother. Its acoustic deficiencies were only finally resolved by the insertion of glass-fibre diffusers in 1968-9.

The long history of the Albert Hall as a concert venue includes such landmarks as the farewell concert of Madame Albani in 1900, the first gramophone concert in 1906 and in 1923, the first performance of Samuel Coleridge-Taylor's musical setting of *Hiawatha*, which became an annual fixture from 1930 to 1940. The Proms moved in in 1941, following the destruction of their original home, the Queen's Hall in Regent Street.

THE NATURAL HISTORY MUSEUM

The idea of a separate national museum of natural history was first mooted by (Sir) Richard Owen (1804-92) in 1856 when he was appointed superintendent of the Natural History department at the British Museum. But the realisation of such a project was bedevilled by the frequent changes of government which characterised the third quarter of the nineteenth century. It was the impossibility of the expense involved in expanding the existing British Museum site in Bloomsbury which had led Owen to propose a wholesale move to South Kensington, where he envisaged it being housed in a vast single-storey complex covering eleven acres. Here the wonders of Creation would be displayed to the general public and explained through free lectures given by the curatorial staff. Owen outlined his scheme in detail in *On the Extent and Aims of a National Museum of Natural History*, which he published in 1862. Interestingly Darwin proved to be a vigorous opponent from the start, partly because he disliked the idea of separating his field of study from the sciences and arts generally and partly because he heartily disliked Owen. Owen found a supporter, however, in Gladstone, a particularly useful ally in that he was an 1851 Commissioner, a Trustee of the British Museum *and* Chancellor of the Exchequer.

The architectural competition for the building was won by the architect of the Albert Hall, Capt. Fowke, who had recently built a natural history museum in Edinburgh. Fowke's death, however, meant that the project was re-assigned to a rising star in his mid-thirties, Alfred Waterhouse (1830-1905). Initially commissioned to implement Fowke's designs – but with leeway to make alterations – Waterhouse jettisoned them almost totally in favour of a bold statement in south German Romanesque of the twelfth century. It was an idiosyncratic choice in an era when High Gothic was all the rage but it was well suited to the decorative display required by Owen. This has been enthusiastically described by John Julius Norwich as "crawling with sculptured animals, living on the left, extinct on the right." But, as Lord Norwich also notes, "On the centre gable, at the suggestion of Prof. T.H. Huxley, there was formerly a carving portraying 'Man: the Greatest

76. The Natural History Museum, designed by Alfred Waterhouse, which opened in 1881.

Beast of All' – as triumphant a proclamation of Darwinism as could be imagined. Alas, it is no longer there."

Changes of government and a surge in building costs obliged Waterhouse to trim his budget radically from £500,000 to £330,000. This meant not only economies in the finish, replacing granite with Portland stone and wooden ceilings with plaster ones, but more importantly major omissions in the facilities, most notably a lecture hall and a library. Plans to raise the sunken site to street level also had to be abandoned. Waterhouse clung tenaciously, however, to his choice of terracotta for the facade, though supplies proved subject to repeated difficulties and delays. These problems, compounded by constant demands for minor changes in the design, meant that construction stretched over seven years (1873-80) and costs actually escalated to £412,000, plus a third as much again for fixtures and display cases. Even so only three departments were ready for the official opening in 1881, the fourth not being completed until 1886.

The Natural History Museum was formally separated from the British Museum in 1963. An eastern extension was completed in 1977. Acclaimed as Museum of the Year in 1980, it unveiled a novel Origin of Species display in 1981. Its library of over 800,000 manuscripts and books is probably the greatest such resource in the world.

THE IMPERIAL INSTITUTE

Architecturally speaking all that remains of the Imperial Institute is a single tower. Organizationally, however, it survives in another distinctive architectural incarnation, the Commonwealth Institute at the western end of High Street, Kensington.

Established to mark Queen Victoria's Golden Jubilee, the Imperial Institute, to paraphrase Dean Acheson, suffered from having an empire but failing to discover a role. The original concept, first mooted in the 1870s, was for some sort of museum or exhibition, a notion which attracted

77. The Imperial Institute in its heyday – the tower alone remains.

the attention of the Prince of Wales, who was himself seeking some sort of public role and doubtless trying, if it did not inconvenience him unduly, to promote projects which would please his royal mother, who still treated him like a potentially delinquent teenager.

In 1880 a reorganized Indian Museum of art objects was opened at South Kensington and in 1886 one of the series of annual exhibitions in the grounds of the Horticultural Society was devoted to the produce of India and the Colonies. Its success re-awakened the notion of some permanent institutional representation of the relationship between Britain and Greater Britain. Once again the Prince of Wales saw a chance to place himself at the head of an initiative which, it was by now clear, the Queen herself warmly favoured. In a letter to the Lord Mayor of London, whom he wished to head a fund-raising drive, the Prince outlined the functions of the proposed Institute as combining those of a museum, an exhibition and what nowadays would be called a think-tank and discussion forum. Its activities would both record the empire's role in promoting 'the arts of civilization' and also positively stimulate trade and emigration, thereby strengthening the bonds of empire.

The fund was duly launched but critics agitated for alternative sites in the City, to give the Institute a business orientation, or Whitehall, to give it a political direction. The Queen, however, saw South Kensington as the appropriate location for what she saw as another embodiment of Albert's idealism. That proved to be one decisive factor. The other was that South Kensington offered a virtually free site.

The organizing committee of the Institute was chaired by Lord Herschell, a past and future Lord Chancellor. Its energetic secretary was Sir Frederick Abel, the inventor of cordite. The committee's restatement of the aims of the new body gave equal weight to representing the products and industries of the United Kingdom itself, an implicit acknowledgment of contemporary anxieties about the need for higher standards of British technical education. The Institute might therefore serve to stimulate scientific research into Empire products and their potential. For the first forty years of its existence this was in practice to be its main contribution to national life.

The design competition for the building was won by T.E. Collcutt, the assessors including Lord Leighton, the President of the Royal Academy, and Alfred Waterhouse, the architect of the adjacent Natural History Museum. Collcutt was a successful and versatile architect whose work was to range from the original Savoy hotel to office-buildings in the City and imposing bourgeois mansions in northern suburbs, like Totteridge, where he lived in one of his own designing. The competition brief for the Institute building specified such conventional facilities as a library and reading rooms, a 'fine reception hall', plus committee and conference rooms and exhibition galleries; but it also required refreshment rooms, emigration offices and store-rooms and laboratories. Collcutt's solution was ambiguously praised as 'a piece of cabinet-making on a colossal scale'. While it was under construction *The Builder* provisionally pronounced the project to be potentially next in importance only to the Houses of Parliament, but its final verdict was damnation with qualified praise, declaring the design to be "entirely refined in detail" with "absolutely nothing of bad or tawdry taste in it" – and yet, and yet ... "we cannot call it a great or striking piece of architecture". The official opening took place in May 1893, but work continued on the building until well into the following year.

Although the fledgling Institute aroused little enthusiasm among the general public, the determination of Sir Frederick Abel that it should serve as a weapon of national value against the rival industrial power of Europe and the USA, ensured that it developed with at least one clear focus and purpose. The intended independence of the Institute was, however, progressively eroded by financial pressures and changes in the institutional landscape. Cost over-runs on the building proved substantial. The rates assessment from the two parishes in which the Institute stood were nearly four times higher than originally estimated. Financial disaster was averted by a variety of expedients. In 1893 a billiard-room was added to the facilities to attract subscribing 'Fellows' with a club-like atmosphere. In 1899 the expanding and recently re-organised University of London took over half the building. In 1901 it was reluctantly acknowledged that the self-imposed central mission of the Institute – to develop the commercial and industrial resources of the empire – basically duplicated a major function of the Board of Trade. In 1902, therefore, the Institute was accordingly placed under the Board's tutelage and functioned essentially as its research department. The exhibition galleries were, however, retained and from that base a new focus and function haphazardly evolved. In 1949 the Institute was transferred to the Ministry of Education in recognition of its educational and cultural activities. Reconstituted as the Commonwealth Institute in 1958, it has developed a wide-ranging programme of work with schools, particularly in the arts and multi-cultural aspects of the curriculum. Expansion of Imperial College led to the demolition of the original Institute building between 1957 and 1965, despite vigorous public objections and the overt regrets of the Royal Fine Arts Commission.

THE VICTORIA AND ALBERT

The origins of the Victoria and Albert Museum – a name it was not to acquire for almost half a century – lie in the Museum of Manufactures established in the aftermath of the Great Exhibition at Marlborough House in September 1852. In 1853 it was re-styled the Museum of Ornamental Art. Meanwhile, at Somerset House, the School of Design, forerunner of the Royal College of Art, had amassed its own collection of plaster casts, engravings and examples of contemporary commercial design. In 1857 the Museum was relocated to premises at South Kensington that were not just new but strikingly novel. Built by leading contractor William Cubitt and opened by the Prince Consort, what became immediately and irreverently known as the 'Brompton Boilers', was, to contemporary eyes, an intimidatingly hi-tech and alien assemblage of cast and corrugated iron and glass. Prince Albert's suggestion of painting the building in the Tudor colours of green and white made it look slightly more user-friendly. While the Museum's collection was arranged in its new home, the School was sidelined to adjacent wooden sheds and the terrace of eighteenth-century houses known as Brompton Park House.

The Director of the new venture, energetic, optimistic Henry Cole, aimed to realise its mission – to promote "the influence of Science and Art upon Productive Industry" – by creating an extensive complex of galleries, halls and premises for learning, lectures and experimentation. At

78. The 'Brompton Boilers', otherwise the original South Kensington Museum, which was eventually relocated to Bethnal Green.

79. The North Court of the South Kensington Museum in 1862.

the core would be "a splendid collection of objects representing the application of Fine Art to manufactures." Cole had already acquired a major collection of pottery and porcelain and to this added examples of design, ranging from ivories, medals and jewellery to glass, furniture and armour, plus items from the Paris Exhibition of 1856. In 1857 Yorkshire clothier John Sheepshanks donated his collection of British art of the last half century, including works by Constable, Etty and Landseer. Francis Fowke was commissioned to design a gallery to house this important acquisition. In that year the institution was organised into departments of Education, Ornamental Art, Construction, Architecture, Animal Products and Food, the latter aiming to promote healthier eating habits, especially among the poor. To ensure that this remained no pious ideal Cole instituted a programme of twice-weekly evening openings, specifically intended for the brief after-hours leisure of the working man and his family. Cole's undoubted flair for public relations and his genuine desire to reach and serve as broad a public as possible also enabled him to attract the services of lecturers as eminent as Ruskin and Thackeray. A Select Committee of 1860 warmly endorsed the museum as a popular and economical venture. In 1862 a new North Court and South Court were opened to take advantage of the publicity and attendance associated with the International Exhibition on the adjacent site.

Further acquisitions and premises to house them were added on to the Sheepshanks Gallery piecemeal, despite a directive of 1863 that "future purchases should be confined to objects wherein Fine Art is supplied to some purpose of utility ... ". The result was that the Museum became, in the apt phrase of its most celebrated modern director, Sir Roy Strong, "a capacious handbag" whose diverse contents reflected the divergence between being "a practical museum of the arts of manufacture and design, with its aim to educate the masses, as against a museum of masterpieces, the resort of antiquarians and connoisseurs." A less tactful contemporary described the collections as looking like a cross between a repository and a craft bazaar. Despite the piecemeal development of both the institution and its premises, 'South Kensington' did achieve both innovation and the ability to harness a range of impressive talents. Owen Jones provided orientalist expertise and wrote the widely influential *Grammar of Ornament*. Edward Poynter became director of the art school. William Morris advised on the acquisition of textiles. Other experts included German architect Gottfried Semper, gifted designer Godfrey Sykes and the versatile sapper Captain Fowke, whose inventions ranged from a folding camera to a new type of door-hinge. There was also a whole detachment of Royal Engineers, whose evolving skills ranged from the speedy erection of cheap temporary buildings to training other branches of the military in applied photography. The firm of Minton, Hollins and Company, with whom Cole was closely linked, effected marvels of majolica and mosaic. Doulton did the same with terra-cotta. Hard-won experience led to significant improvements in gallery design, notably in the use of iron as both a constructional and a decorative material. The museum also featured Britain's first gas-lit gallery. Through its programmes of art education, moreover, South Kensington had a nationwide impact, enhancing in particular the employment opportunities of gifted women, a cause particularly dear to Cole himself, who did not scruple to employ his own female relatives. In the decoration of its buildings, moreover, the museum was also able to employ such outstanding artistic talents as Leighton, Watts and Prinsep; but the outstanding achievement of the early period was, perhaps, the Green Dining Room, created by Morris, Marshall, Faulkner and Co. in 1868-70.

In 1867 the 'Brompton Boilers' were largely demolished and in 1872 transferred to Bethnal Green to house the first museum collection expressly intended for the working classes. Dire predictions of drunken rampages were confounded by the orderly and appreciative behaviour of East Enders. Now revamped as the Museum of Childhood, Bethnal Green remains an out-station of the V. & A.

The transfer of the contents of the India Museum from the India Office added a substantial non-European dimension to the South Kensington Museum. The opening of the National Art Library there in 1884 made it clear that the existing premises had to be rationalised and extended. In 1890 eight architects were invited to submit designs for a new building. From these Sir Alfred Waterhouse recommended the work of the youthful Aston Webb. It was not until 1899, however, that the foundation stone of the new building was laid by Queen Victoria, who used the occasion to direct that henceforth the South Kensington Museum should be known as the Victoria and Albert Museum. It was to prove to be the aged sovereign's last public engagement. Aston Webb's building was opened a decade later by Edward VII. In the same year the museum passed to the control of the Board of Education.

THE SCIENCE MUSEUM

The science department at South Kensington developed as something of a poor relation of the ever-proliferating arts side. Its somewhat miscellaneous collections included left-overs from 1851, the contents of the Patent Office's own museum, Fowke's Construction gallery and unique relics of major historic significance such as Arkwright's spinning jenny and the locomotive 'Puffing Billy'. If there was a unifying theme it was machinery and the history of invention. Overshadowed by the (literal) rise of the Natural History Museum, science, despite the dogged efforts of such stalwarts as T.H. Huxley and Sir Henry Roscoe (*see p. 105*) and educationists Sir Lyon Playfair (*see p. 105*) and James Kay-Shuttleworth, failed to find an institutional home commensurate with its widely admitted standing or comparable with what already existed in Paris. Changes of government, Treasury parsimony, the jealousy of rival institutions and what Huxley denounced as "simple ignorant cussedness", chiefly of civil servants, combined to delay even the appointment of an overall Director to the Science Museum as an institution in its own right, until 1893. The opening of the reconstructed V. & A. in 1909 offered an historic opportunity to hive off the science collections physically; but construction work on the Science Museum's own building did not begin until 1914 and its formal opening did not take place until 1928. Delay, at least, had the advantage of enabling it to enlarge its sphere of coverage to embrace new disciplines such as electrical engineering and oceanography. The construction of the adjacent Geological Museum was undertaken between 1929 and 1933, enabling that institution to vacate cramped but valuable premises in Jermyn Street.

Worlds of Learning

The creation of Albertopolis might perhaps be thought to have, almost inevitably, made 'South Kensington' a powerful lodestone for learned societies and institutes of higher learning. But its association with scholarship, in its less exalted forms at least, pre-dated this evolution by a century. Like Stoke Newington or Hackney on the east side of London or Clapham and Camberwell on the south, in the mid-eighteenth century the area was sufficiently removed from the tumult and temptations of the metropolis to qualify, almost by default of those qualities alone, as a self-evident grove of academe. Even more to the point, it was cheap. That was certainly the major thrust of a newspaper advertisement of 1748 on behalf of Hull's Academy, informing prospective patrons that it had "Removed from Hampstead Heath to the Great House at Earl's Court near Kensington, lately in the possession of the Russian Ambassador." Noting that the "exorbitant Prices of School-Masters in and about Town" had provoked parents into despatching their offspring to "distant counties" for instruction, Hull's Academy offered to square the circle of inexpensive remoteness and conveniently located competence, offering a curriculum of no less than twenty-one subjects and skills for just ten guineas a year. Another newspaper advertisement, of 1756, for a young ladies' boarding-school at ' Brompton Park ' – possibly the terrace known as Brompton Park House (*see p. 16*) – confirms that Hull's Academy was not an isolated venture. More specialised instruction was offered at Lewis Lochee's military academy in Little Chelsea, at what is now 240-48 Fulham

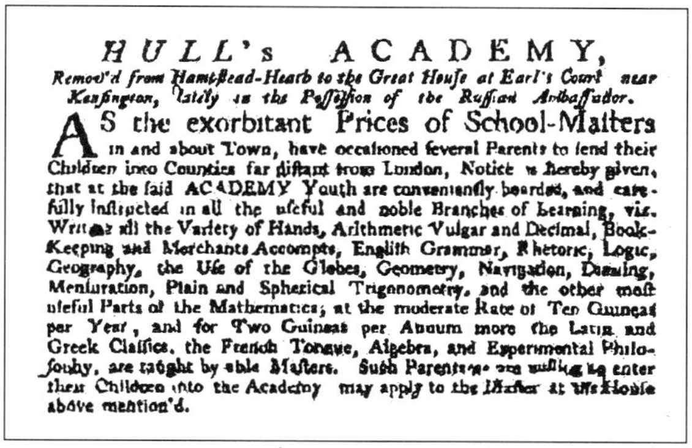
HULL's ACADEMY,
Remov'd from Hamſtead-Heath to the Great Houſe at Earl's Court near Kenſington, lately in the Poſſeſſion of the Ruſſian Ambaſſador.

AS the exorbitant Prices of School-Maſters in and about Town, have occaſioned ſeveral Parents to ſend their Children into Counties far diſtant from London, Notice is hereby given, that at the ſaid ACADEMY Youth are conveniently boarded, and carefully inſtructed in all the uſeful and noble Branches of Learning, viz. Writing all the Variety of Hands, Arithmetic Vulgar and Decimal, Book-Keeping and Merchants Accompts, Engliſh Grammar, Rhetoric, Logic, Geography, the Uſe of the Globes, Geometry, Navigation, Drawing, Menſuration, Plain and Spherical Trigonometry, and the other moſt uſeful Parts of the Mathematics; at the moderate Rate of Ten Guineas per Year, and for Two Guineas per Annum more the Latin and Greek Claſſics, the French Tongue, Algebra, and Experimental Philoſophy, are taught by able Maſters. Such Parents as are willing to enter their Children into the Academy may apply to the Maſter at the Houſe above mention'd.

81. Advertisement for Hull's Academy in Earl's Court (1748) in a house it claims to have been the residence of the Russian Ambassador.

80. Blemell House School opened in 1819 on the future site of the Brompton Oratory (see next page).

Road, from 1770 onwards (*see ill. 83*). A very early balloon ascent took place there in 1784, perhaps an enterprising publicity stunt to boost the institution. Lochee closed the academy in 1789 and was killed in an opening skirmish of the revolutionary wars in the Low Countries. The poet, Laetitia Landon (*see pp. 24-5*) was educated at a private academy in Hans Place, run by two French ladies, where her classmates included Caroline Lamb, who was later to become infatuated with Lord Byron.

Once Brompton began to thicken out in population it began to need larger local schools to cater for the children of local residents. Blemell House School (*ill. 80*), a privately-owned venture, opened in 1819 on the future site of the Brompton Oratory, where it continued in business until the site was sold to the Oratorians. The Western Grammar School was established in 1828 on the site of what was then part of Harrison's nursery and is now Alexander Place. The school was organised as a distinctly new kind of proprietary venture, in which parent power was allegedly guaranteed by shareholder status in a joint-stock company under the presidency of Sir Theophilus Lee, a local resident. Its committee included the local writer William Jerdan and local architect W.F. Pocock but emphatically excluded local actor J.B. Buckstone. For four years the teaching followed the Madras or Lancastrian system whereby a single master instructed monitors who in turn instructed the pupils. This trickle-down system proved more ineffective than cost-effective and was abandoned in favour of more 'ancient' modes of pedagogy. Between 1835 and 1839 purpose-built school buildings were erected to designs by W.F. Pocock. In 1836 the school was deemed sufficiently meritorious to establish an association with the newly-founded King's College of the University of London, a linkage which necessitated that the teaching staff should be Anglicans and that the school's religious teaching should be that of the established church. A surviving Doric section of the school buildings was converted to become two houses in 1927-9, the school having finally closed down in 1912.

The Brompton National School, another Anglican institution, was established in 1841-2 as a satellite of Holy Trinity, Brompton in a building on the site of the former 'Melon Ground', designed by George Godwin junior and built by James Bonnin junior. It catered for two hundred boys and two hundred girls and in 1890 transferred to the former Brompton Chapel, where it remained until 1939, the premises subsequently being taken over by Bonham's. Another National school was established around 1850 in the former almshouses (themselves built on the site of a former pest-house) in Gore Lane, a straggle of some fifty cottages south of Kensington Gore.

From 1870 church schools were supplemented by publicly-funded Board Schools. The London School Board built one in Clareville Street in 1880-81, both street and school then being known as Gloucester Grove East. Renamed Bousfield School in 1913 in honour of a former chairman of the school managers, it moved to newly-built premises in The Boltons in 1957 and its old buildings were taken over by Our Lady of Victories Roman Catholic Primary School.

Many other small and ephemeral establishments are known to have existed. In 1854 there was an 'Oral Educational Institute' at 41 Onslow Square. There were two boys' preparatory schools in Hereford Square. An 1888 issue of the St. Mary Abbot's parish magazine carried notices for Harrington House school for girls at 30-31 Philbeach Gardens; Cromwell House School at 54 Hogarth Road; a kindergarten and preparatory school at 58 Penywern Road; a prep school for boys at 2 Harrington Gardens; another school for 7s-13s at 10 Collingham Gardens; and, at 1

82. All Saints School in Brompton Road near Knightsbridge. An opportunist fast-food stall stands in attendance.

83. A school of valour – Lochee's Military School at what is now 240-48 Fulham Road.

Trebovir Road, Trebovir House School, which numbered among its pupils the daughters of actresses Ellen Terry and Mrs. Patrick Campbell and the future novelist Marguerite Radclyffe Hall.

Similar private sector ventures continued into the twentieth century. In 1910 Earl's Court Square had a dancing school and an army tutor. In 1914 Marguerite Vacani founded a school of dancing and deportment in Harrington Gardens which initiated not only debs but, from the 1930s children as well, into the mysteries of coping with curtsies, trains and fans, numbering among its pupils both the Queen and Princess Margaret.

Cosmopolitan dimensions are, at the time of writing, represented locally by the Institut Français and Lycée Charles de Gaulle, the Goethe Institute and the presence of the overseas programmes of American universities such as Boston (Harrington Gardens), Pepperdine (Exhibition Road) and Samford (Ashburn Gardens).

84. A lecture at Mrs Louise Jopling's Art School in South Kensington. From the Daily Graphic 20 Feb, 1891.

CARLISLE & GREGSON

(JIMMY'S) LTD.

Have for over 70 years specialised in coaching for the Services and University Entrance and Honours Examinations

NAVAL CADETSHIPS
ROYAL INDIAN NAVY
NAVAL PAYMASTER CADETSHIPS
ROYAL MARINES
SCHOOL CERTIFICATE and UNIVERSITY EXAMINATIONS

Hours of Work: 9.30 a.m. to 1.30 p.m.
and 2.30 p.m. to 4.30 p.m.
Mondays to Fridays inclusive
(Saturdays, mornings only)

85. A 1930s advertisement for Carlisle & Gregson's naval school in Lexham Gardens, off Earl's Court Road.

For Practical Training in
THE DANCE
and
THE ARTS OF THE THEATRE
apply to
THE
GINNER MAWER SCHOOL
of
DANCE AND DRAMA

86. Advertisement for the Ginner Mawer School of Dance and Drama in Philbeach Gardens c.1937.

IMPERIAL COLLEGE

The student body of Imperial College could claim to be markedly cosmopolitan, thus reversing in a way its original purposes and signification, which were to maintain and denote British imperial dominance, rather than to reflect the diversity of its now former possessions overseas. Imperial College is a constituent school of the federal University of London but has long been large enough and certainly eminent enough to rank as a university of international standing in its own right. True to the vision of the Prince Consort, as interpreted by Cole in the role of high priest of the cult of public improvement, Imperial's Royal Charter required it "to give the highest specialised instruction and to provide the fullest equipment for the most advanced training and research in various branches of science, especially in its application to industry."

Imperial was formed in 1907-10 by the merging of three institutions. The Royal College of Science had evolved from the Royal College of Chemistry established in 1845 under the presidency of the Prince Consort. Its most celebrated teacher was 'Darwin's bulldog', T.H. Huxley, its most celebrated student science-fiction pioneer H.G. Wells. The Royal School of Mines dated from 1851. The proximity of these two schools to one another at South Kensington led to close co-operation from the 1880s, the decade in which they were joined physically, though not yet institutionally, by the City and Guilds College, a creation of the City of London and, in no small measure, of local residents Roscoe and Playfair. Its main strength lay in the complementary field of engineering. The merger of the three institutions was motivated by increasing fear of German technological superiority, specifically exemplified in the state-of-the-art Berlin Technical High School. Cross-party consensus united some of the keenest political minds of the age in support of this initiative, notably ex-Premiers Rosebery and Balfour, Germanophile reformer Lord Haldane and the socialist founder of the London School of Economics, Sidney Webb.

Faith and Worship

HOLY TRINITY CHURCH, BROMPTON

Holy Trinity was designed in a spare Early English Gothic idiom by Thomas Leverton Donaldson, built in 1826-9 and extended by Sir Arthur Blomfield in 1879-82. From 1749 the site had been used as a burial ground for poor patients from St George's Hospital at Hyde Park Corner. That part of the site not actually used for burials yielded vegetables for the hospital's patients. As originally consecrated, Holy Trinity was to serve a large area, stretching west to the Kensington Canal and north to the Kensington Turnpike. The first incumbent, Percival Frye, exemplified Anglican nepotism at its most literal, being the nephew of Archdeacon Pott, the Vicar of Kensington. Contemporary critics condemned the finished building as plain to the point of ugliness. An avenue of trees was planted down to Brompton Road in 1831, softening at least the main approach. In 1843 local architect John Blore added tracery to the aisle windows and embellished the chancel. *The Builder* still judged the exterior 'most unsightly'. In 1863 a font designed by local resident E.C. Hakewill was installed, along with a circular stained glass window as a memorial to Stroud Lincoln, a churchwarden and lawyer who had played a prominent role in raising finance for the development of Alexander Square and Pelham Crescent. Blomfield's alterations were matched by the addition of a new organ and pulpit and stained glass for the chancel windows. In 1885 an Italian-made reredos of gold mosaic, designed by J. R. Clayton of Clayton & Bell, was installed. Numerous further extensions were made at the behest of A.W. Gouch, vicar from 1899 to 1931. The churchyard was closed as early as 1854. In 1871 a small infants school was donated by the builder Charles Freake. The 'church house' of 1965 is on its site.

87. Holy Trinity, Brompton, by T.H. Shepherd.

88. The construction of the dome of the second Brompton Oratory in 1880. Architect Herbert Gribble died before it was completed.

THE BROMPTON ORATORY

The Oratory of St Philip Neri and the Immaculate Heart of Mary commemorates an Italian mystic who founded a congregation of secular priests in 1564. The London presence of the Institute of the Oratory dates from shortly after its introduction to England by Cardinal Newman in the 1840s. The site of the present church was acquired in 1853, when the Renaissance-style house of the Oratorians was erected to the designs of the prominent Catholic architect J.J. Scoles. It was not, however, until 1880 that construction of the present church began. The youthful, unknown designer Herbert Gribble (1848-94), a pupil of local resident J.A. Hansom (*see p. 77*), worked in conscious imitation of the mother church of the order in Rome, the Chiesa Nuova, built by St Philip Neri himself. Gribble's purpose, frankly declared, was "so that those who had no opportunity of going to Italy to see an Italian church had only to come here to see the model of one." Pevsner judges the result to be "London's most thoroughgoing nineteenth century import of the Italian style"; it has also been characterised more briefly as "a Baroque time-warp". Numerous gifts from continental Europe have enriched the interior – the Twelve Apostles by Giuseppe Mazzuoli, a pupil of Bernini, came from Siena cathedral; the spectacular altar of 1693 is from Brescia and another altar, of the early eighteenth century, from Maastricht. In 1896 a statue of Cardinal Newman, by L.J. Chevalliaud, was erected outside. The steel-framed main dome was completed in the same year. The marbling, gilding and mosaics added by Commendatore Formilli between 1927 and 1932 have been characterised by Harwood and Saint as being "of defiantly Roman taste" – which would certainly be true to the self-confident Counter-Reformation spirit of the original. In 1938 the gifted Rex Whistler painted a triptych depicting English martyrs. The funeral of Cardinal Manning took place at the Oratory in 1892. It was London's premier Catholic church until Westminster Cathedral opened in 1903 and remains famed for its music.

89. Brompton Oratory.

ST MARY, THE BOLTONS

Built in 1849-50 to the designs of George Godwin the Younger (*see p. 78*) St Mary's, West Brompton as it was initially known, was largely paid for by the first incumbent, the Revd Hogarth Swale, the site being donated by George Gunter. *The Ecclesiologist* lambasted the location of the stone pulpit under the open lantern as irredeemably low church and condemned the aiseless cruciform layout as a mere "auditorium disguised". External angels around a squat spire later added a whimsical touch. Significant alterations were made by Joseph Peacock in 1870-2 and by Romilly Craze in 1952, when most of the Victorian fittings were removed to make way for whitewashed austerity. St Mary's was the first church in the area whose catchment was carved out of the large area initially assigned to Holy Trinity, Brompton.

W.T. Du Boulay, vicar from 1868 to 1909, introduced a decidedly more Ritualist mode of worship and established a 'Guild of St. Michael' for the benefit of local female domestics, who were encouraged to renounce fairs, races, dancing and music halls.

90. St Mary's, The Boltons in 1850.

ST PAUL'S, ONSLOW SQUARE

Consecrated in 1860, St Paul's was built on a site donated by the Smith's Charity trustees to designs by James Edmeston, church architect and hymn writer. Freake, the builder, was patron of the living and is commemorated by a memorial tablet. During the long (1876-1909) incumbency of Hanmer Webb-Peploe St Paul's became a noted centre for Evangelicalism. Substantial embellishments were made to the church in 1888-9, most notably the insertion of stained glass windows depicting scenes from the life of St Paul, made by Clayton & Bell. Other acquisitions included oak pews, a pulpit of Caen stone and a brass eagle lectern. St Paul's was united with Holy Trinity, Brompton in 1977.

91. The Revd Webb Peploe, incumbent of St Paul's, Onslow Square, 1876-1909.

ST PETER'S, CRANLEY GARDENS

Erected in 1866-7 to designs prepared in Freake's own office, St Peter's also stood on a site donated by Smith's Charity. The first organist there until 1871, was none other than the composer (Sir) Arthur Sullivan. The congregation, according to one incumbent, "always had a large number of knights" and a backbone of retired service officers and officials – "Not great men perhaps, not of the first rank, but faithful servants of the State, men who had done something." The large and prosperous congregation funded two major schemes of improvement in 1907-9 and 1922-3 by the phenomenally prolific W.D. Caroe (1857-1938), a pupil of John Loughborough Pearson and architect to the Ecclesiastical Commissioners. A major restoration was undertaken again in 1958 but the last Anglican service was held in 1973 when the parish was united with that of St Mary's, The Boltons. In 1975 St Peter's was reconsecrated to become the cathedral church of London's Armenian community.

ST AUGUSTINE'S, QUEEN'S GATE

St Augustine's was a High Church project, headed by the Reverend Prebendary W.J. Irons, vicar of Holy Trinity, Brompton. He and his supporters began by looking for a site in the area of Hereford Square but found themselves effectively pre-empted by the establishment of St Peter's in Cranley Gardens. Persevering, they finally acquired a site in what was then an undeveloped area south of Queen's Gate, paid for by J.A. Shaw Stewart M.P., a leading member of the project steering committee and a co-founder of Keble College, Oxford. Their choice of architect was William Butterfield (1814-1900), a fervent disciple of Pugin and designer of Keble College, Oxford and of the flamboyant All Saints, Margaret Street. St Augustine's was to be his last major London church. Surrounded by serried ranks of stuccoed terraces – which Butterfield despised – St Augustine's was, in composition and choice of materials, as the *Survey of London* notes drily, "designed without regard to adjacent buildings." Elizabeth and Wayland Young characterise the result as "a rather quiet Butterfield church as they go. The outside is only moderately amazing; it is set slightly at an angle to the street frontage and has absolutely square shoulders with only a small belfry for tower in the middle. But the shoulders are so high that the effect is deeply striking." Building began in 1870 but was not substantially completed until

92. St Augustine's, c.1905 – "only moderately amazing".

1877. With a parish population of only around three thousand to support its maintenance Butterfield's swan-song was to prove more than they could cope with. Major repairs were needed in 1917 and again in 1920, when a chunk of the ceiling fell in. A partial restoration of Butterfield's original polychrome decor was made in 1974-5 but some areas had been so thoroughly whitewashed in the 1920s that a complete exposure of all the stripes and zig-zags proved impossible.

ST LUKE'S, REDCLIFFE SQUARE

Built in 1872-3 to designs by George Godwin and his brother Henry this expensive structure featured rich carving and Minton tiles. The expense of the project was a key factor in pushing the contracting firm of Corbett and McClymont into bankruptcy. The church's own subsequent financial problems ensured that few alterations were made to it subsequently.

OUR LADY OF SEVEN DOLOURS

The Church of Our Lady of Seven Dolours and St Mary's Priory of the Servite Friars covers a narrow but deep site at 264 Fulham Road. Around 1650 a single house and garden stood there. From 1681 to 1700 it was the home of Nicholas Staggins, Master of the King's Musick. It subsequently became a school and between 1836 and 1868, when it was known as Heckfield Lodge, was occupied by the Miltons, a military family. What remains of Heckfield Lodge now forms the core of the Priory. The Servites – members of the Order of the Servants of Mary – came to England in 1864 and bought the Fulham Road site in 1873. Construction began the following year, the architects being J.A. Hansom and his son J.S. Hansom. The foundation stone was laid by Cardinal Manning. Altar panels in a thirteenth-century style were contributed by a resident, Father Simoni.

ST CUTHBERT'S, PHILBEACH GARDENS

St Cuthbert's parish was carved out of St Philip's, Earl's Court Road but spiritually it was an offshoot of St Matthias, Warwick Road, which had already established one daughter church, St Patrick's, in Kenway Road, in 1872. Housed in an iron shed St Patrick's proved to be a temporary venture, never replaced after it burned down in 1879. In 1882 St Cuthbert's also started in an iron structure, referred to affectionately by some members of its congregation as 'the dust-bin'. It also faced opposition from the Bishop of London, who thought the proposed parish did not have enough poor people in it. And there was a problem of financing, which meant that it was built largely on bank loans and by fits and starts. Its promoter, the Revd Henry Westall, who remained the incumbent until his death in 1924, proved indefatigable.

The architect was Hugh Roumieu Gough (1843-1904), an experienced professional who had, with the more talented J.J. Seddon, recently completed St Paul's, Hammersmith. Gough modelled the

93. The Philbeach Hall attached to St Cuthbert's, built 1894-6.

proportions of St Cuthbert's on Tintern Abbey. Westall, mindful of the church's dedication to the great Northumbrian pioneer of monasticism, obtained a foundation stone from Lindisfarne.

St Cuthbert's was finally consecrated in 1887 but that marked only a beginning, not an end. From then until the outbreak of the Great War Westall ceaselessly chivvied his affluent congregation to give not only their money but also their time and personal labour to embellish the raw new church. Organized into pseudo-medieval 'Guilds' and guided by professional craftsmen, they carved, painted and embroidered to the glory of the Lord. Their efforts, in the words of the *Survey of London* "turned an impressive but unoriginal building into a monument to turn-of-the-century Anglo-Catholic taste rivalled in London only by Holy Trinity, Sloane Street." "

The elaborate pulpit of Caen stone was the work of a professional, Baron Felix de Sziemanowicz, who also carved the sedilia and piscina. The most important single contribution, however, was made by a member of the congregation, as Ian Nairn recognised: "What lifts the church into being something special is the glittering talent of Bainbridge Reynolds... Here, for once is a genuine English Art Nouveau, and an inventiveness equal to that of Mackintosh ... "

In 1894-6 the adjacent Philbeach Hall (*ill. 93*) was added, comprising such facilities as a meeting-hall, gymnasium, library and six suites of rooms for bachelor curates.

St Cuthbert's soon became celebrated for the elaborateness of its ritual as well as of its decor. It was to be the first Anglican church in which the Host was reserved. On Good Friday 1898 the ceremonial 'Adoration of the Cross' was interrupted by an unseemly scuffle with Protestant agitators. This demonstration, and Westall's imperturbability throughout it, served only to raise his standing. Although the leader of the protest, John Kensit, was acquitted of criminal behaviour, Westall had his revenge by having Kensit's portrait carved on one of the misericords in the chancel – complete with the ears of an ass.

HOLY TRINITY, PRINCE CONSORT ROAD

Projected in 1899 to serve the residents of the new apartment blocks rising around it, Holy Trinity was an initiative of H.B. Coward, vicar of Holy Trinity, Knightsbridge. He and his supporters encountered what one might reasonably call the usual opposition from churches already established locally, on the grounds that a new one would be superfluous and the population of its proposed parish at 2,500 too small. This inevitably led to difficulties in raising finance. The promoters persisted and succeeded, enlisting as their architect the distinguished G. F. Bodley (1827-1907), who had been responsible for cathedrals in Tasmania and Washington D.C. Bodley, undeterred by the irregularity of the site, intended to produce "a town church in the style and manner of the fourteenth century". It was to be his last work, consecrated in 1903 and completed in the year of his death.

THE CHRISTUSKIRCHE

From 1781 until 1901 a German Lutheran congregation held services at the Queen's Chapel of St James's Palace. Edward VII discontinued this practice in 1902 and it was left to Baron Schroder of the banking dynasty to rescue the homeless congregation by building them the Christuskirche in Montpelier Place, Knightsbridge. The foundation stone was laid on 25 June 1904, the anniversary of the 1530 Confession of Augsburg, drawn up by the German theologian Melancthon as a moderate statement of Lutheran doctrine. The consecration service was held in November, and Kaiser Wilhelm II donated silver, marked with the imperial monogram.

94. The German Lutheran Christuskirche in Montpelier Place, consecrated in November 1904.

Architects and Builders

W.F. Pocock (1779-1849) designer of the Western Grammar School (1835-9) in Alexander Place, was the son of a London builder and, as an architect, was more distinguished by his writing than by any major project. A founder member of the Royal Institute of British Architects, in 1807 he published *Architectural Designs for Rustic Cottages*, which went to further editions in 1819 and 1823. He also produced a book on the design of chapels and others on room finishings and brick bonding patterns. Pocock died at Trevor Terrace, Knightsbridge. W.W. Pocock (1813-99) was responsible for building Ovington Square between 1844 and 1852.

Anthony Salvin (1779-1881) scion of an ancient Durham lineage, developed a lucrative niche in the architectural profession as a specialist in castle restorations. His list of projects reads like a guide-book – The Tower of London, Windsor Castle, Carisbrook, Caernarfon, Bangor, Durham, Warwick, Alnwick ... not to mention numerous manor houses. Salvin also designed at least nine churches and four schools, as well as parsonages, hotels and Gurney's Bank in Norwich. A Fellow of the Society of Antiquaries from his twenties, Salvin also became Vice-President of the Royal Institute of British Architects. From 1865 until his death he divided his time between his town house at 19 Cranley Place and his country retreat at Hawksfold, Fernhurst near Haslemere.

The early career of Joseph Aloysius Hansom (1803-82) was dogged by disappointment. The son of a York joiner, he was initially apprenticed to his father but, on showing a talent for drawing, was released to train under a local architect. After designing churches in Liverpool, Hull and the Isle of Man, Hansom was commissioned to build Birmingham's huge neo-classical town hall, an enterprise which bankrupted him when he stood surety for the contractor. While supervising this project Hansom lived a short cab drive away at 27 Sumner Place (1873-77). He died at 399 Fulham Road. Hansom is generally credited with inventing the cab which was named after him, for which he received an unprofitable patent in 1834. But his design was ungainly and what we think of now as a hansom cab was almost certainly designed by the unsung John Chapman. The inventive Hansom also founded and edited the early issues of *The Builder* (*see* George Godwin below). His architect son, J.S. Hansom, maintained 27 Thurloe Street as his office until 1913.

Charles James Richardson (1806-71), another pupil of Soane, lived at 22 Brompton Crescent from 1842 until 1850, during which time he was master of the architectural class in the school of design at Somerset House. In 1852 he designed a mansion for the Earl of Harrington in Kensington Palace Gardens. Richardson, an expert on subjects as various as Tudor architecture and

95. Hansom cab (left) outside the cabmen's shelter in Kensington Gardens.

heating and ventilation, bequeathed a collection of over five hundred drawings by prominent British architects to the then South Kensington Museum (the later V & A).

In 1841 Royal Academy architectural student Edward Charles Hakewill (1812-72) was living at 17 Alexander Square in the home of his father, the architect to Rugby School. Between 1854 and 1867 Hakewill junior lived at 8 Thurloe Square. A pupil of Philip Hardwick, Hakewill was a competent technician, rather than an architectural star like Basevi, and eventually became a metropolitan district surveyor. He left Thurloe Square to retire to Suffolk, where his brother John had had a provincial practice.

William Railton (died 1877), who lived at 65 Onslow Square from 1858 until his death, is best remembered as the designer of Nelson's Column. A pupil of William Inwood, he followed literally in his mentor's footsteps by studying in Greece. From 1838 to 1848 Railton served as architect to the Ecclesiastical Commissioners, designing numerous churches.

George Godwin the Younger (1815-88) was born in Brompton, the son of local architect George Godwin (1786-1863), to whom he was apprenticed at thirteen. At twenty Godwin *fils* won the first medal ever awarded by the Royal Institute of British Architects, for an essay on concrete which was immediately translated into several languages and was long regarded as a standard authority on the topic. At twenty-one Godwin was instrumental in founding the Art Union of London to promote higher standards of public taste. At twenty-five he published a two volume work on *The Churches of London*. In 1844 he took over the editorship of *The Builder* and raised it to become the preeminent journal of the construction trades. In its pages he campaigned for sanitary reform, better housing for the poor and higher ethical standards in a business notorious for cutting costs and corners to the detriment of both employees and customers. A man of wide cultural interests, Godwin took an active role in the Royal Literary Fund, supported efforts to establish a national theatre and became a Fellow of both the Royal Society and the Society of Antiquaries. In old age he served on the 1884-5 Royal Commission to investigate the housing of the working classes and was awarded the Gold Medal of the Royal Institute of British Architects. Godwin's lifelong hobby was collecting chairs said to have belonged to

96. George Godwin the Younger, the conscience of his profession.

97. Godwin's memorial in Brompton Cemetery. The central panel bears his portrait.

the famous – including Anne Boleyn, Shakespeare, Raleigh, Pope, Mrs Siddons, Byron, Napoleon, Thackeray, and Trollope. Godwin's local work included Brompton's parochial national school, St Mary's church, The Boltons, St Jude's church, Earl's Court, and the handsome villas of Redcliffe Gardens, Tregunter Road and The Boltons. From 1847 to 1872 Godwin lived in his father's former home at 24 Alexander Square, then moved to Cromwell Place where he died. He was buried in Brompton cemetery (*ill. 97*).

Sir George Gilbert Scott (1811-78) built up the largest architectural practice in England. After his death *The Builder* published a list of 732 projects on which he had acted as architect, restorer or consultant. The most famous include the Albert Memorial, St Pancras station hotel and the Foreign Office. By the time Scott retired to 39 Courtfield Gardens in 1877 he was still supervising the rebuilding of St. Mary Abbot's, Kensington. Scott was buried in Westminster Abbey, where he had himself carried out extensive restorations. Two of his sons, George and John Oldrid, followed him into architecture, as did his grandson, Sir Giles Gilbert Scott, designer of Battersea and Bankside power stations and the red telephone kiosk.

Herbert Gribble (1847-94), designer of the Brompton Oratory, lived at 10 Alexander Square in the early 1880s and from 1883 until his death at 64 Redcliffe Road, presumably to be near to the major project of his life while it was under construction. A Devonian by birth, he had trained at the National Art Training School of the Science and Art Department in the Museum adjacent to the Oratory site and had been a pupil of local resident J.A. Hansom, working for him on the church of St Philip Neri at Arundel.

Sir Edwin Lutyens (1869-1944), designer of the Cenotaph and of dozens of handsome country residences, grew up in the house of his painter father at 16 Onslow Square. Lutyens was commissioned to produce designs for several projects in the Kensington area – none of which was ever built. The earliest was a studio to be built in Wetherby Place, behind Hereford Square, the grandest were designs for a new Institut Français in Queensberry Place and a National Theatre on the Cromwell Road. Lutyens did add a music room to the back of 49 Gloucester Road for the publisher Adam Black.

98. The architectural practice of Ernest George and Harold Peto did much work in Brompton, including the magnificently ornate houses in Harrington Gardens. Harold Peto himself lived at 10 Collingham Gardens, which was featured in a series depicting architects' own homes.

Artists and Sculptors

MASTERS IN BRONZE

Born in Turin, Baron Carlo Marochetti (1805-67) was honoured by the royal houses of both Italy and France but, as a consequence of the revolutions of 1848, found England – specifically 34 Onslow Square – a more congenial place of residence. Marochetti established his local reputation with a monumentally heroic representation of Richard the Lionheart, cast for the Great Exhibition of 1851. It was greatly admired by Prince Albert, who personally selected its now permanent location outside the Houses of Parliament. Marochetti's other prominent London landmarks include statues of the two greatest railway engineers of the age, I.K. Brunel and Robert Stephenson, which stand at Temple and Euston station respectively, and the brooding figure of Highland hero Sir Colin Campbell in Waterloo Place. He was also responsible for casting the lions designed by Sir Edwin Landseer to complement Nelson's Column and was Victoria's first choice to design the statue for Albert's memorial, though death cheated him of that commission. If Marochetti won royal favour, public esteem eluded him. The artistic establishment dismissed his work as 'flashy'. *Punch* lampooned him consistently as 'Count Marrowfatty'.

99. Baron Carlo Marochetti.

Nearby Sydney Mews off the Fulham Road housed a complex of workshops which included Marochetti's studio and foundry – where Landseer's Trafalgar Square lions were cast. After his death the premises were skilfully and extensively converted to become Avenue Studios, whose tenants constitute a positive roll-call of late Victorian and Edwardian artistic talents – Boehm, Poynter, Gilbert, Singer Sargent, Steer and Tweed among them.

Unlike Marochetti, Sir Joseph Edgar Boehm (1834-90) came to enjoy both royal and popular admiration, with the result that he bore an English rather than a foreign title. Boehm was born in Vienna, the son of the director of the Austrian Mint, but he was educated in England and opted to settle for good in 1862. As a German-speaker,

100. Terra-cotta sculptures outside Boehm's house at 25 Wetherby Gardens.

101. Princess Louise, close friend and possibly lover of Sir Joseph Boehm.

gifted with a suave and polished manner, he became a favourite with the royal family and served as advisor (and, many also believed, lover) to Victoria's daughter, Princess Louise, a more than competent sculptor in her own right. Boehm even impressed the short-tempered 'Sage of Chelsea', historian and critic Thomas Carlyle, who had a low opinion of artists in general. Boehm's Chelsea Embankment statue of the Scottish curmudgeon, lounging in his dressing-gown and surrounded by piles of books, was greeted with praise by contemporaries. The poet Robert Browning moved a vote of thanks to the artist at its unveiling in 1882.

For Boehm the 1880s proved a decade of triumph. In 1881 *Vanity Fair* profiled him enthusiastically: "He has produced a marvellous amount of work and all of it good; for he knows what he means to express and how he means to express it. He has furnished many statues to India and the Colonies. He delights in quadrupeds, and especially in horses, many of which he has modelled, and one of which he rides every morning at daybreak. He is much admired by the Royal Family. His manners are excellent and his companionship altogether pleasant and profitable. He is a very good man of business." In 1882 Boehm completed his statue of Lord Lawrence, hero of the Indian rebellion of 1857. In 1884 he produced a convincing, if somewhat idealised, monument to William Tyndale, first translator of the entire Bible into English. Tyndale is shown beside a printing press, which Boehm, with typical thoroughness, based on a sixteenth-century example he had found in Antwerp. The subject is also swathed in academic robes, which he is most unlikely to have worn in everyday life, but to which he was, indeed, technically entitled and in which, in Boehm's opinion, Tyndale's weighty scholarship required that he should be shown. In 1885 Boehm, who had initially taken over Marochetti's house and lived at 78 Cromwell Gardens since 1874, moved into his newly built house at 25 Wetherby Gardens. The classical columns of its porticoed entrance are decorated with flamboyant terra-cotta panels designed, and signed, by the artist himself. In 1887, the year of Victoria's Golden Jubilee, a new coinage was issued, based on Boehm's designs. In 1888 Boehm's statue of the Duke of Wellington was unveiled at Hyde Park Corner. His next major commission was to honour a contemporary icon, Lord Robert Napier. He never lived to complete it, dying suddenly at the age of fifty-six. According to his protégé Alfred Gilbert, who completed the Napier commission, Boehm's abrupt demise was precipitated by an amorous encounter with Princess Louise in the Fulham Road studios which the two men shared.

Sir Charles Wheeler (1892-1974), who lived at 21 Tregunter Road in the 1930s, was a protégé of the architect Sir Herbert Baker who arranged for his first commission, a memorial plaque commemorating John Kipling, the poet's only son, killed in action within days of arriving at the front. The aftermath of the Great War provided many further memorial commissions but by the 1930s Wheeler was engaged on the project for which he was to be chiefly remembered, a series of statues and bronze doors for the Bank of England, then nearing the end of a wholesale reconstruction under Baker's direction. Elected A.R.A. in 1934, a Fellow of the Royal Society of British Sculptors in 1935 and R.A. in 1940, Wheeler served as President of the Royal Academy from 1956 to 1966.

102. Sir Charles Wheeler at work.

103. Sir John Everett Millais.

BRUSH WITH FORTUNE

Sir John Everett Millais (1829-96) began as the archetypal artistic rebel and ended as the President of the Royal Academy, claiming to be the highest-paid artist in history. Born to a Jersey family, he became at eleven the youngest ever student to enter the Royal Academy Schools. He exhibited for the first time when just seventeen. When he was nineteen he became a founder-member of the self-consciously radical Pre-Raphaelite Brotherhood, which was established at the home of his parents in Gower Street, Bloomsbury. Two years later Millais became a national sensation with his portrayal of *Christ in the House of his Parents*, a painting rich in theological symbolism but also remarkable for its realistic depiction of the Holy Family. The picture moved some critics, notably Dickens, to paroxysms of disgust. But John Ruskin, the leading art critic of the day, defended the painting, the painter (potentially "a second Turner") and the P.R.B. Millais eventually reciprocated by relieving Ruskin of his wife. In 1868 Millais moved into 7 Cromwell Place (now the home of the National Art Collections Fund), where he was to paint one of his most widely reproduced canvases, the fanciful *Boyhood of Raleigh*. Millais moved on to more palatial premises in 1872. In 1885 he was elevated to a baronetcy and on his death was honoured with interment in St Paul's.

Walter Severn (1830-1904), eldest son of John Keats' devoted companion, Joseph Severn, was a professional civil servant in the education department, reserving his artistic career to his leisure hours and retirement. A protégé of John Ruskin and a close friend of Charles Eastlake, the first director of the National Gallery, Severn worked to revive interest in the ancient crafts of art needlework and embroidery but himself excelled in watercolour landscapes. In 1865 he was instrumental in founding the Dudley Gallery, which attracted the support of such major figures as Edward Burne-Jones and G.F. Watts. Severn's work features in galleries in Sydney, Melbourne and Adelaide. He died in Earl's Court Square.

Arthur Hughes (1832-1915) exhibited prize-winning promise as a teenager at the Royal Academy schools, became a disciple, though not a member of the Pre-Raphaelite Brotherhood, and even modelled for Millais as *The Proscribed Royalist*. Content with work and family, Hughes lived an unspectacular, almost reclusive, life, attracting little general attention to his accomplished paintings, many of which passed straight from his studio into the hands of an appreciative circle of private collectors. Hughes reached a wider public through his book illustrations. While living at 2 Finborough Road between 1869 and 1877 he produced illustrations for *Tom Brown's Schooldays* and for two volumes of verse by Christina Rossetti. He also served for a decade as an examiner at the South Kensington Art Schools.

Elizabeth Southernden, better known as Lady Butler, (1846-1933) trained at South Kensington School of Art and in Rome. Her painting *The Roll Call* (1874) brought her instant celebrity when it was bought by Queen Victoria, establishing the artist as par excellence a delineator of military subjects. Military men who may have cared little for art as such were warmly appreciative of the accuracy with which she reproduced uniforms and weaponry. Critics applauded her skill in composition and the excellence of her depictions of horses and men in violent action and movement. Married to Major – later Lieutenant-General Sir – William Francis Butler in 1877, the artist and her husband moved to 3 Tregunter Road the following year. Here she painted *The Remnants of an Army* (1879), now in the Tate Gallery, and, a highly topical subject, *The Defence of Rorke's Drift* (1880), now in Windsor Castle. Despite the technical excellence of her work and its lasting popularity, Lady Butler was never elected even an Associate of the Royal Academy, being passed over in 1879.

The financially and socially successful career of Sir John Lavery (1856-1941) now receives short shrift in the *Oxford Companion to Art*. Born in Belfast, Lavery was a member of the Glasgow School before moving on to London and Paris. He finally settled at Cromwell Place in a house opposite the home of Millais. Lavery's depiction of *The Royal Family at Buckingham Palace*, exhibited at the Royal Academy in 1913, may seem a stiff and artificial composition almost a century later but at the time it was praised as "a veritable triumph over the formalism to which in such pictures we are accustomed ... the urbanity that links royal persons with the other gentlefolk of England is well seized." It can now be seen in the National Portrait Gallery, as can his 1931 portrait of Ramsay Macdonald.

The career of Sir William Newenham Montague Orpen (1878-1931), in terms of an alleged failure or betrayal of early promise, almost parallelled that of Lavery and is similarly dismissed by the *Companion* as that of "a brilliant, prolific and somewhat superficial painter, the most successful artist of his day." Born in Co. Dublin, Orpen studied at the Dublin School of Art and then at the Slade. His 1900 debut portrait of fellow student Augustus John was a superb study of scruffy student arrogance, tinged with a jaunty loucheness. A founder member of the anti-Establishment New English Art Club, Orpen became Establishment enough to serve as an official war artist, as official recorder of the post-war Paris Peace Conference and as portraitist of Prime Minister Lloyd George. Knighted in 1918, he was elected R.A. the following year. Orpen lived at 8 South Bolton Gardens from 1906 until his death and is commemorated in the name of Orpen House, an apartment block in Trebovir Road.

Irish-born Francis Bacon (1909-92) also occupied the house of Sir John Millais at 7 Cromwell Place, but, unlike his distinguished predecessor, remained an *enfant terrible* all his life. Arguably the most internationally renowned British painter of the twentieth century, Bacon had no formal training and worked throughout the 1930s as an interior designer. In 1944 he committed himself wholly to painting, destroying almost all of his earlier work, a gesture of typical flamboyance. A brashly assertive and hard-drinking homosexual, Bacon became a notorious Soho 'character' in the 1950s. Bacon himself described his often violent canvases as the product of 'exhilarated despair'. His iconic status as an epitome of self-destructive genius is attested by the tribute portraits of Lucien Freud, R.B. Kitaj and photographer Bill Brandt. The inclusion of Bacon's works in the films of Bertolucci and Pasolini affirm the cultural resonance of his work far beyond the shores of his adopted country.

ARTIST BY DESIGN

Godfrey Sykes (1825-66) was a product of the government school of art at Sheffield and a disciple of Ernest Stevens. Recruited to assist Capt. Fowke in designing terra-cotta columns for the Royal Horticultural Society's garden, he showed himself to be a master not only of that medium but of ironwork and majolica as well. In the few brief years in which he worked in the area Sykes came to exert a decisive influence on the development of a distinctive South Kensington style, as evidenced by his work on the North and South Courts of the museum building, the Prince Consort Gallery, the columns of the lec-

104. Cromwell Place, c.1905, home to fashionable society portraitist, Sir John Lavery.

ture theatre and the decor of the Refreshment Room, completed by his pupil James Gamble. At Thackeray's request Sykes also designed the cover of the *Cornhill Magazine*. Sykes died at Old Brompton and was buried in Brompton Cemetery.

THE CARTOONISTS

Illustrator Richard Doyle (1824-83) was trained by his father, the political cartoonist John Doyle (1797-1868), and revealed an early talent for playful and grotesque fantasy. A regular contributor to newly-founded *Punch* magazine from the age of nineteen, Doyle was also responsible for designing its famous cover, depicting Mr. Punch with his dog, Toby. Doyle, a staunch Catholic, broke all ties with *Punch* in 1850 as a result of its virulent campaign against the re-establishment of a Roman hierarchy in Britain. Although he contributed to the *Cornhill Magazine* under the editorship of Thackeray Doyle turned henceforth mainly to book illustration, most notably for Ruskin's *King of the Golden River* and Thackeray's *The Newcomes*. He also produced fine water-colours of rural landscapes in Devon and Wales. Doyle lived at 7 Finborough Road from 1875 until his death. A well-liked member of the Athenaeum and friend of Planché, Doyle's personality was such that the normally strait-laced *Dictionary of National Biography* memorialised him as "a singularly sweet and noble type of English gentleman" and asserted whimsically that "in Oberon's court he would at once have been appointed sergeant-painter."

Bruce Bairnsfather (1888-1959) is best remembered as the creator of the indefatigable Great War veteran 'Old Bill'. Born in India the son of a professional soldier, Bairnsfather himself left the army to become a representative for a firm of electrical engineers; drawing and performing as an amateur comedian were relegated to his spare time. Rejoining his regiment during the Great War, Bairnsfather made Old Bill a national institution and the inspiration for a West End revue and a play. Relatively speaking the rest of Bairnsfather's career as a cartoonist, comedian and lecturer was an anti-climax, although he did also serve as an official cartoonist with US forces in Europe 1942-4. Bairnsfather lived at 1 Sterling Street.

Novelists

Jane Austen (1775-1817) made a protracted visit to her brother Henry at 23 Hans Place in the years 1814-15, a time when the composition of *Emma* was drawing to a close and work on *Persuasion* just beginning. Surrounded by metropolitan sophistication, she still believed that, as she confided in a letter written in September 1814, "three or four families in a country village is the very thing to work on". Her admirer Sir Walter Scott certainly agreed, praising her work in the *Quarterly Review* in 1815.

The roller-coaster life of William Makepeace Thackeray (1811-63) would have qualified him for inclusion as a character in one of his own novels, a man self-destroyed by his own fecklessness, failures and ill-fortune. Born to luxury in India, he was packed off to England at six. A brutal education, culminating at Charterhouse ('Slaughter House') left him with temporary baldness and a permanently broken nose. Thackeray then left Cambridge without a degree, having inconveniently gambled away an inheritance prior to actually inheriting it. But he had made lifelong friends of Tennyson and Edward Fitzgerald and seemed to have many gifts to fall back on – he could draw well, sing well and even fence well. But, after failing successively as a lawyer, an editor, an artist and a foreign correspondent, and having lost the rest of his capital in an Indian banking smash, he found himself at twenty-six a married man with an infant daughter but no certain future. Lacking other assets, he had no option but to persevere with his pen as another daughter was born – and died – and then yet another, the arrival of which plunged his wife into an irreversible mental breakdown. Isabella Thackeray was confined to asylums until her death, half a century later. Thackeray's daughters were sent to Paris, where they could live more cheaply with his mother.

Alone once more, Thackeray set to repairing his fortunes by contributing occasional pieces to whichever periodical would accept them, but salvation finally came through a profitable association with newly-founded *Punch* magazine and the publication of his finest novel *Vanity Fair* (1847-8). Success enabled him to reunite his family and take a modest but comfortable house with double bow-windows in Young Street, Kensington. Freed from financial worry at last, Thackeray could afford to indulge himself and revel in his

105. William Makepeace Thackeray.

celebrity, reeling, as he himself said, 'from dinner party to dinner party – I wallow in turtle and swim in claret and Shampang'.

Lobsters, jam tarts, good cigars and fine claret were among his favourite indulgences. Before the lease on Young Street ran out Thackeray moved on to 36 Onslow Square, which was to be the Thackeray family home from 1854 until 1861. This was to prove an eventful period, though overshadowed by the curse of his failing health. Thackeray completed *The Newcomes* in 1855 and followed it with a lecture tour of the United States, which yielded material to be incorporated into *The Virginians* (1857-9). In 1857 he fought a by-election at Oxford, losing by only a few score votes. In 1860 he became the first editor of the *Cornhill Magazine*. Under his guidance it rapidly established a reputation for literary excellence which was to sustain it for over a century.

Thackeray, a tall and powerfully built man with an imposing shock of silver hair, found himself increasingly incapacitated for work by the cumulative impact of years of irregular hours and excessive eating and drinking. Bouts of violent retching left him totally exhausted. A urethral affliction, probably contracted during his Bohemian days as an art student in Paris, brought further recurrent pain. He found consolation in the attentive care he received from his affectionate daughters and in 1861 showed his appreciation by removing them from Onslow Square to the splendour of an architect-designed palazzo, 2 Palace Green, Kensington. He died there, suddenly, on Christmas Eve 1863. The funeral, at Kensal Green cemetery, was attended by two thousand people; mourners included fellow novelists Dickens and Trollope, poets Browning and Tennyson and the entire staff of *Punch*.

Marie Corelli (1855-1924) became the best-selling English female novelist of her day, loathed and despised by literary critics, but numbering among her fans Oscar Wilde and Prime Minister Gladstone, who once spent two hours ensconced with her at 47 Longridge Road, while Mrs Gladstone waited outside in their carriage "to enjoy the fresh air". Born the illegitimate daughter of Charles Mackay, a song-writer and sometime editor of the *Illustrated London News*, Mary Mackay was educated by governesses and initially trained as a concert pianist. Hopes of a musical career were abruptly dashed when her father was struck down by illness. Mary, reincarnated as Marie, determined to save her family by becoming a famous novelist – and did. Moving into Longridge Road with her stricken father in 1883, she had already vindicated her gamble by the time he died in 1889. By 1901 Corelli was wealthy enough to remove to Stratford-upon-Avon, where she continued to churn out further titles, although her literary standing collapsed well before her death.

When the future Sir Henry Rider Haggard (1856-1925) moved into 24 Redcliffe Square in 1888 he had but recently completed the trio of novels for which he is best remembered – *King Solomon's Mines* (1885), *She* (1887) and *Allan Quatermain* (1887). Many more were to follow but none approached the success of these early 'ripping yarns', which won him the friendship of Kipling and the admiration of Jung. Haggard moved from Redcliffe Square in 1891 and in his later years researched and wrote extensively and sensibly on agricultural and imperial issues such as forestry and emigration policy.

E.F.Benson (1867-1940) was the son of an Archbishop of Canterbury and the brother of A.C. Benson, literary biographer and composer

106. Longridge Road, home to Marie Corelli – the Earl's Court wheel is in the background.

107. H. Rider Haggard.

of *'Land of Hope and Glory'*, and of R.H.Benson, the Roman Catholic apologist. Edward Frederic Benson lived at 25 Brompton Square for the last two decades of his life, during which he produced the most successful and enduring works of his prolific *oeuvre*. His series of novels featuring the ludicrous social rivalries and absurd cultural pretensions of Mapp and Lucia were set in Rye, where Benson had his country home, Lamb House, the former residence of Henry James. Adapted for television, 'Mapp and Lucia' found new and appreciative audiences in the 1980s.

In his own day Ronald Firbank (1886-1926) was dismissed by all (except, notably, the Sitwells) as a literary butterfly – a motif which constantly crops up in his novels. In retrospect he has been hailed as a stylistic innovator to rival Joyce and a seminal influence on writers as eminent and diverse as Evelyn Waugh and Muriel Spark. A sickly child, Firbank was educated at home until he was fourteen. After a spell in France to acquire the language, he lived in 1905-6 at 49 Nevern Square while being tutored for the diplomatic service examinations. In career terms this all came to nothing. Its real outcome was Firbank's first publication *Odette d'Autrevernes*. It was published at his own expense, as were all his works until 1924. He could afford to indulge himself, being the son of an MP and a society beauty and the grandson of a millionaire railway contractor. At Cambridge he became a friend of Vyvyan Holland, Oscar Wilde's son, and was received into the Roman church by R.H. Benson. Firbank was to prove anything but religious, but he maintained a life-long adoration of Catholic ritual. He left Cambridge without a degree but bequeathed it the memory of his room – draped with red silk and filled with candles, lilies and iconic portraits of his mother.

Dandyism came naturally to Firbank but was reinforced by his admiration for Wilde and Beardsley, whom he imitated by patronising the Café Royal or Soho restaurants in spectacular solitude. Sleekly pomaded hair and a dusting of face-powder enhanced the cadaverousness of his features. Jewelled rings, crimson finger-nails and the constant carrying of a cane and gloves drew attention to his elegant hands. His calculated eccentricities included writing his novels on stacks of blue postcards and growing a palm tree in his apartment and paying a gardener to come in twice a day to water it. In 1912 Firbank lived with his adored mother at 102 Queen's Gate but passed the Great War in seclusion at Oxford, though he did also keep a suite of rooms in Pall Mall as a London *pied a terre*.

Dennis Wheatley (1897-1977) had already sold the lucrative family wine business in Mayfair by the time he moved into 48 Queen's Gate in 1931. During the five years that he lived there he established his best-selling credentials with his first novel *The Forbidden Territory* (1933) and with *The Devil Rides Out* (1934) struck a rich vein – Satanism and the occult – which he was to mine profitably for decades. Wheatley also went on to write spy stories, initially set against the contemporary background of the Second World War and then, through the character of Roger Brook, Mr Pitt's secret agent, against the canvas of the French Revolution and Napoleonic periods. On being told that Wheatley's novels had been translated into every European language bar one the critic and novelist Pamela Frankau instantly observed that the missing one must be English. Wheatley would doubtless have laughed – all the way to the bank.

Georgette Heyer (1902-74) became Jane Austen

reincarnated with 'attitude'. In her novels feisty heroines and dashing heroes overcome adversities to find true love in the colourful Regency period, of whose manners, idiom and lifestyle Heyer acquired an undisputedly expert knowledge. She found her métier with *Devil's Cub* (1934) and *Regency Buck* (1935). The latter includes a description of Tattersall's (*see p. 136*), where the heroine, Judith Tavener, is taken by her aristocratic guardian to buy a matched pair of carriage-horses. Heyer also developed a parallel interest in detective novels in both contemporary and historical settings. In *Duplicate Death* her ex-con heroine Beulah Birley lives in a flat off Cromwell Road, just where Heyer and her barrister husband had their first marital home.

New Zealand-born Ngaio Marsh (1899-1982) divided her career between the theatre and the detective novel and her life between London and her native land. While living in Montpelier Walk in "a little house ... on the sunny side of the street, looking towards the dome of the Oratory", she became a regular patron at the nearby Prince of Wales pub. The Oratory becomes 'Baronsgate Basilica' in *Black as He's Painted*. The tangle of streets, squares and mews around her home became 'the Capricorns', a stylish enclave populated by such distinctive characters as the retired diplomat Whipplestone, the spinster proprietress of an '*École de Dance*', Lucy Lockett, a kleptomaniac cat and two fat Africans who run the strangely sinister Piggy Potterie. Just around the corner in 'Palace Park Gardens '(?Prince's Gardens) is the Ng'ombwana embassy, temporary residence of its head of state, familiarly known as 'The Boomer' to Marsh's regular hero Superintendent Roderick Alleyn, a prep school pal of the said potentate. Marsh also lived for a season in the Rembrandt hotel, opposite the V & A, and in the 1930s ran a highly successful gift shop on the Brompton Road. When it moved to larger premises in Beauchamp Place it unaccountably flopped. Marsh herself lived there in the 1950s with a student secretary and used it as a location in *A Surfeit of Lampreys*, when the Lampreys, returning from New Zealand, move into a flat there to economize on living expenses.

Brigid Brophy (1929-95) was the daughter of novelist John Brophy (1899-1965), a Liverpudlian veteran of the Great War who lived at 59 Coleherne Court in the 1950s, when she, newly down from Oxford, had her first major success with *Hackenfeller's Ape* (1953). The story of a laboratory animal that takes on human characteristics, the book exemplified two of the writer's enduring preoccupations – experimentation with fantasy and a ferocious commitment to the crusade against vivisection. As the leading member of the Writers' Action Group, she was also largely responsible for the establishment of Public Lending Right for British authors. Brophy lived at Flat 3, 185 Old Brompton Road, with her husband, art historian Sir Michael Levey, Director of the National Gallery, from the 1960s until the early 1980s, when the onset of multiple sclerosis obliged her to move. Her illness provided subject-matter for a further collection of essays, whimsically entitled *Baroque 'n' Roll* (1985).

By the time he moved into 199 Cromwell Road in 1964 C.P. Snow (1905-1980) had definitively arrived at the heart of the British Establishment. His personal odyssey, from son of a Leicester church organist to eminent academic and trusted government adviser, provides the central theme for his autobiographical eleven-novel series, *Strangers and Brothers*, composed over a thirty year period between 1940 and 1970. Its narrator, Lewis Eliot, a lower middle-class barrister, finally penetrates what Snow called in one of his titles the *Corridors of Power* (1963). Snow himself did so as Parliamentary Secretary at the Ministry of Technology (1964-6) and a Labour Life Peer (1964). While living at Cromwell Road Snow completed the *Strangers and Brothers* sequence with *The Sleep of Reason* (1968) and *Last Things* (1970) and published a critical biography of Trollope (1975). His wife Pamela Hansford Johnson (1912-81) meanwhile completed her 'Dorothy Merlin' trilogy, satirising the pretensions of literary life, with *Cork Street, Next to the Hatters* (1965). In 1975 they moved to 85 Eaton Terrace.

Musical People

HARMONIOUS IMPORTS

The market for music in eighteenth- and nineteenth-century London proved far greater than native talent could supply and the metropolis consequently attracted a steady trickle of Continental performers and composers, notably from Italy and Germany. Muzio Clementi (1752-1832) came to England at fourteen with the wealthy Beckford family. After seven years in Dorset he came to London, rapidly establishing his reputation as a piano virtuoso. After conducting the Italian Opera in London from 1777 to 1780, he toured extensively in Europe and shrewdly invested in piano manufacturing and music publishing businesses, using his travels to promote these as well as his performing career. A prolific composer, Clementi produced four symphonies and sixty piano sonatas and a hundred progressive piano studies. Clementi lived at 10 Brompton Lower Grove between 1826 and 1828 and is buried in Westminster Abbey cloisters.

Elizabeth Billington (?1765/8-1818) (née Weichsel) was born in Soho, her father a German oboist, her mother a singing pupil of J.C. Bach. Her own precocious talents led her to perform as a pianist at nine before she turned to singing. Teenage marriage to double-bass player James Billington proved unhappy but did not prevent her from studying under the greatest voice teachers of the age with immense diligence to become, according to the *Dictionary of National Biography* nothing less than "the greatest singer England has ever produced". Sir Joshua Reynolds evidently endorsed this view long before it had been written, painting her as St Cecilia, patron saint of music. In 1792-3 Billington was living at 16 Michael's Place but scandal arising from the publication of what were allegedly her *Memoirs* forced her to flee abroad for most of the next decade. Following the death of her husband she contracted a second, even more disastrous, marriage in Italy, but this did not prevent her from returning to the London stage in 1801, commanding a fee of 3,000 guineas for the season, plus a benefit concert guaranteed at a minimum £500. In fact she made between £10,000 and £15,000. By 1805 she was back in Michael's Place, this time at number 33. In 1806 Billington produced *La Clemenza di Tito,* the first Mozart opera to be presented in England. Leaving Michael's Place in 1807, she retired from the stage in 1811.

John Braham (really Abraham) (1774-1856), the son of German Jewish immigrants, was orphaned in childhood, 'discovered' at the Ashkenazi synagogue in Duke's Place, Aldgate and adopted by the Jewish musician Leoni, who gave him a thorough musical education. Having made his debut as a treble at thirteen, Braham eventually turned tenor. A tour of Europe gained the patronage of Josephine Beauharnais and the friendship of Elizabeth Billington, for whom he subsequently appeared in her pioneering production of *Clemenza.* Returning to England Braham began to compose as well as perform, receiving a thousand guineas for his first opera. Constant appearances in London and assiduous touring of provincial festivals accumulated an immense fortune which he dissipated disastrously by buying the Regent's Park Colosseum for £40,000 in 1831 and building the St James's Theatre for £30,000 in 1835. Both projects failing commercially, Braham was forced to return to the stage in his sixties, though his voice had been seriously damaged by abuse. Well-liked as a conversationalist and having friends as exalted as the cultured Duke of Sussex, Braham throughout his career dismayed both the critics and his acquaintances by flashy and meretricious displays of vocal virtuosity unworthy of his extraordinary natural gifts. Braham rented Brompton Grange, Yeoman's Row from 1830 to 1842 and retired to The Grange, Brompton in 1852, dying there in 1856.

The career of Jenny Lind (1820-1887) has an almost fairy-tale quality in representing the seemingly irresistible rise of a divinely gifted innocent from poverty and obscurity to great wealth and even greater fame. Born Johanna Maria Lind in Stockholm, she was sent to the court theatre school at nine and made her operatic debut at eighteen. Her voice proved remarkable not only for range but also for purity. Her vocal agility and breath control were likewise considered extraordinary. She could sing simple ballads with fervour but was also capable of composing virtuoso cadenzas for herself. Within a decade both Meyerbeer and Verdi were writing roles specifically for her. Lind's London debut in 1847 sent the city "mad about the Swedish nightingale". Success, however, failed to convince her that the operatic stage was really respectable and in 1849 she retired from opera with some relief to devote herself to oratorios

108. *Jenny Lind.*

and the concert platform, specialising in music both sacred and sentimental. In 1850 she toured the USA under the management of flamboyant showman P.T. Barnum. Barnum was more used to promoting dwarves, bearded ladies and two-headed cows but he could recognise a superstar when he saw one. Three-dollar seats at the concerts he arranged were said to change hands for seventy-five times as much.

In 1852 Jenny married her accompanist Otto Goldschmidt and in 1856 they settled in London, where he founded a Bach choir in which she led the sopranos. From 1876 to 1886 they lived in some style at 189 Old Brompton Road. In 1883 Jenny made her last public appearance, typically in a charity concert, and in that same year became Professor of Singing at the Royal College of Music. She gave up her teaching there in 1886, moving to Malvern, where she died the following year. Her monument in Westminster Abbey is just below that of Handel and both appropriately bear the inscription *"I know that my Redeemer liveth."*

TO THE NEW WORLD

German composer and refugee from Nazism Kurt Weill (1900-50) lived in a tiny flat in Bramham Gardens, Earl's Court from January to July 1935 while working on a musical called *A Kingdom for a Cow*. It failed dismally. This disappointment was, however, more than compensated for by his reconciliation with his ex-wife, Lotte Lenya, with whom he then emigrated to the USA.

Hungarian composer Bela Bartok (1881-1945), who settled in the USA in 1940, regularly stayed at 7 Sydney Place whenever he was performing in London. Bartok's First Violin Sonata, performed on the occasion of his first visit to London in 1922, was dismissed by a leading critic of the day as "the last word (for the present) in ugliness and incoherence". Subsequent opinion has been more positive, his string quartets in particular being hailed as the best since Beethoven.

NATIVE TALENTS

Cornish-born tenor Charles Incledon (1763-1826) was sent at eight to sing in the cathedral choir at Exeter but ran away to sea at sixteen. After seeing action with the Royal Navy, he was encouraged by his officers to turn his natural

109. *Charles Incledon.*

musical talent to professional advantage. After a slow start in the provinces Incledon made his London debut at Vauxhall Gardens in 1790. By 1800 he was starring in the first British performance of Haydn's *Creation* at Covent Garden, where he became a leading light, alongside Mrs Billington. At the height of his fame, from 1802 to 1811, Incledon lived at 13 Brompton Crescent. Ballads, rather than opera, suited him best because he failed to develop as an actor, being handicapped by a poor memory and a vulgar accent. Vulgarity seems, indeed, to have been a hallmark of his character, extending to his speech, manner and dress, to the distaste of fellow professionals, such as Charles Mathews the elder. Less fastidious personalities found Incledon genial, generous and witty.

Soprano Dame Emma Albani (1847-1930) was born near Montreal, christened Marie Louise Cecile Emma Lajeunesse. After studying in Paris and Milan she made her debut at Messina in 1870 and appeared in London in 1872. In 1878 she married operatic impresario Ernest Gye. From 1879 to 1898 they lived at 16 The Boltons, from 1899 at Park House, whose site is now occupied by 227 Earl's Court Road and at 61 Tregunter Road from 1908 until her death. Emma Albani was the first Canadian-born artist to achieve international fame in opera and concert singing. By the time she retired from the stage in 1896 she had sung forty-three leading roles. She continued to tour in concert for another decade.

LIGHTENING CONDUCTOR

Sir Malcolm Sargent (1895-1967), who lived at Albert Hall Mansions, came to enjoy a particularly close rapport with the audiences who gathered to hear him conduct next door. Sargent won the Sawyer Prize at the Royal College of Organists at fifteen and as assistant organist at Peterborough Cathedral from 1911 to 1914 underwent an exacting apprenticeship. After service in the First World War, he took his D. Mus. at Durham in 1919. For a while he flirted with the idea of becoming a concert pianist or even a 'second Elgar'. He first conducted when his tone-poem *Rhapsody on a Windy Day* was performed at a Promenade concert in 1921 and his success on that occasion – as conductor rather than composer – fixed the course of his life. In 1923 he was invited to join the staff of the Royal College of Music. In 1928 he became conductor of the Royal Choral Society and in 1950 of the BBC Symphony Orchestra. Sargent took over direction of the Proms in 1948, bringing to his own performances not only a brilliant technique but also the flair of an instinctive showman. As a panelist on the BBC's *Brains Trust*, he impressed not only as an artist but as a personification of the decent, commonsensical Englishman – an impression rather at odds with his platform image as the svelte 'Flash Harry'. The sheen of Sargent's success obscured such personal reverses as a severe tubercular illness which cost him two full years in the 1930s and the death from polio of his much loved daughter in 1944. He bore his own final months with exemplary grace, dying a few days after an unforgettable farewell at the last night of his beloved Proms. Few can have done more to encourage popular appreciation of classical music.

THE SWINGING SIXTIES

Lying in the hinterland of the King's Road, Chelsea, the Brompton area proved a convenient location for many of the rock and pop idols of the capital's most culturally frenetic decade.

The aptly named Troubadour Coffee Shop at 265 Old Brompton Road proved a popular hang-out with musicians. Bob Dylan performed there on his first trip to England and it was here that Alexis Korner recruited drummer Charlie Watts to play for his band Blues Incorporated, through whom Watts met the rest of the Rolling Stones.

The Beatles burst upon the world in 1963, appearing twice at the Albert Hall. On the first occasion Paul McCartney met future girlfriend Jane Asher, who had come to interview him on behalf of the *Radio Times*. In the same year the Beatles several times went to parties at 3 Montpelier Square, the home of Victor Lownes, owner of the Playboy Club.

In 1964 Rod Stewart was living in Reece Mews in the home of Long John Baldry, who had recruited him for his band, The Hoochie Coochie Men, after hearing Stewart play his mouth-organ at Twickenham railway station. Meanwhile the late Ian Dury was studying at the Royal College of Art and in Flat 1 at 10 Gledhow Gardens the youthful Andrew Lloyd Webber was writing *Jesus Christ, Superstar*. Webber knew the area well, having been brought up at Harrington Court (since demolished). Later he was to buy a house at 37 Brompton Square.

In 1966 Jimi Hendrix played his first London engagement at Blaise's, 121 Queen's Gate. (The building was demolished in 1992). 1966 was also the year in which Brian May and Roger Taylor both entered Imperial College, the former to read physics and astronomy, the latter biology. As guitarist and drummer respectively for Queen they became so rich that in the 1970s May was able to return to the area and buy a house in nearby Queen's Gate Terrace. In the same year Brian Jones, living at 1 Courtfield Road, was writing *Ruby Tuesday* with Keith Richard. A car crash at the traffic lights at the junction of Redcliffe Gardens and Old Brompton Road inspired John Lennon to write *A Day in the Life*: "*I read the news today, about a lucky man who made the grade. He blew his mind out in a car. He didn't know the lights had changed.*" The driver, Tara Browne, was a friend of Lennon's, driving a Lotus Elan while high on LSD.

David Bowie was another who chose to return – to The Boltons, no less – when he could afford to move up-market. In 1967-8 he lived at 22 Clareville Grove in the attic bedsit of his then girlfriend, picturesquely named Hermione Farthingale. Bowie subsequently referred to her as "the girl with the mousy hair" in *Life on Mars*. It was while living at Clareville Grove that he wrote *Space Oddity*.

In 1968 the neighbourhood was positively overflowing with pop personalities. Eric Clapton played his last concert with Cream at the Albert Hall. Yes, living in Drayton Gardens, were writing *The Yes Album*. Syd Barrett, having just parted from Pink Floyd had found shelter at Egerton Court, 4 Old Brompton Road, in the apartment of Storm Thorgerson, designer of album covers for the group, an occupation which now sounds as antediluvian as hand-loom weaver.

Album covers were, however, icons of the age – Ian Dury had been taught by the designer of the Beatles' *Sergeant Pepper* cover. The Rolling Stones, who wanted to launch *Beggar's Banquet* in a sleeve covered with lavatory graffiti were obliged by their record company to accept something rather less gratuitously offensive. They had their revenge at the promotion party held at the Gore Hotel, 109 Queen's Gate, where they pelted Decca executives with cake and drink.

Although the sixties now seem the stuff of legend, a tradition lingered on. Phil and Don Everley opted for the Albert Hall for their reunion concert in 1984 and in the 1990s the small but exclusive Franklin Hotel at 28 Egerton Gardens remained a favourite stop-over venue for the likes of Sting and Tina Turner.

THE ROYAL COLLEGES

The Prince Consort envisaged the establishment of an institution devoted to music with a permanent home in South Kensington as early as 1853 but nothing practical was done until 1865 when Henry Cole, acting through the Royal Society of Arts, convened a committee under the chairmanship of the Duke of Edinburgh, to enquire into national standards of music. As expected and intended, it recommended the establishment of a national training scheme for music. Initially the hope appears to have been that the Royal Academy of Music would undertake such a role and agree to relocate to South Kensington. The Royal Academy proved obdurate in its resistance to either proposal. In 1873 it was finally decided to establish a training school independent of the R.A.M. Given a free site, Cole's friend and neighbour, speculative builder Charles Freake, offered to construct the building at his own risk. It was designed, free of charge, by Cole's eldest son, Lt. H.H. Cole R.E. The extensive sgraffito decoration was the work of another Cole protégé, F.W. Moody. Cole thought the design, with its bold oriel windows, strongly reminiscent of fifteenth century England. Subsequent commentators have thought it looked as though it would have been more at home in Venice or even Istanbul. Contemporaries liked it very much and a century later Pevsner still praised it as "delightfully fresh ... quite unlike any other public building of its date". It certainly fulfils one of the fundamental design criteria – that it should in no way resemble the adjacent Albert Hall.

The National Training School for Music was opened in 1876 with the composer (Sir) Arthur Sullivan as Principal. In the same year the School was superseded by the Royal College of Music whose first Director was George Grove, editor of the encyclopaedic dictionary of music named after him. Cole's building soon proved too small and between 1889 and 1894 a new home was built nearby on Prince Consort Road to the designs of Sir Arthur Blomfield. The site, valued at £45,000, was secured on a 999 year lease at £5 a year. The building was paid for by a Leeds ironmaster, Samson Fox. Unfortunately for him he became the subject of a sustained journalistic campaign by Jerome K. Jerome. Best remembered as the author of that genial idyll of the Thames *Three Men in a Boat*, Jerome was at that stage a crusader against capitalist sleaze. Fox took him to court for libel only to be awarded

symbolic damages of a farthing. So – no title for him.

In the year of the building's completion Grove was succeeded as Director of the Royal College of Music by (Sir) Hubert Parry, best remembered for his 1916 setting of Blake's *Jerusalem*. At the same time the collector Sir George Donaldson presented the College with three hundred historical instruments, including Haydn's clavichord and Handel's spinet and a guitar which belonged to Mary Queen of Scots' music teacher, David Rizzio. Distinguished students of the new College were to include the composers Ralph Vaughan Williams and Benjamin Britten and the diva Dame Clara Butt. Cole's original building, meanwhile, remained untenanted between 1896 and 1903. It was then assigned to the Royal College of Organists, which had been founded in 1863, but previously housed only in a series of makeshift homes in Bloomsbury.

110. (Left) The National Training School, now used by the Royal College of Organists.

111. (Below) The Royal College of Music.

Stage and Screen

THE BROMPTON SQUARE SET

As early as 1850 Peter Cunningham, the author of the *Handbook of London*, could say of Brompton that "it has long been and is still the favourite residence of actors and singers."

One of the first to settle in was George Colman the Younger (1762-1836), who lived at 22 Brompton Square from 1825 until his death. The son of a dramatist, he benefited from the same elite education as his father – Westminster and Christ Church, Oxford. Colman's father also helped to launch his career by staging his first plays and in 1794, the year of his death, had the satisfaction of seeing his son succeed him as manager of Covent Garden. Talented as both an actor and author, the younger Colman proved far less stable than his father as a man of business. However, despite a clandestine marriage and a career characterised by a penchant for low comic roles, personal profligacy and a reckless urge to pursue expensive litigation, Colman was, perhaps surprisingly, appointed Examiner of Plays in 1824. A latecomer to respectability, he vindicated his sponsors by his conduct in office. As the *Cambridge Guide to English Literature* puts it - "As an administrator of censorship he earned considerable resentment, exercising a prudery in judgment at odds with his own work." No. 22 Brompton Square was subsequently, in 1849-51, 1856-7 and 1861, the home of actor James Vining (1795-1870), who also lived at 21 Pelham Crescent in 1847-9, 1852 and 1862-7. Initially a Shakespearian, Vining came to specialize in lovers and fops but in old age played Dr Manette in a stage version of Dickens' *A Tale of Two Cities*. Vining's brother, Frederick (?1790-1871), a versatile comedian, lived at 21 (now 5) Pelham Place in 1841-4. James Vining's neighbour, at 20 Pelham Crescent from 1860 to 1867 was John Cooper (?1800 -1870) who once played Iago to Kean's Othello but was essentially a utility actor, better known for his versatility and conscientiousness than his brilliance.

Melancholic in his private disposition, John Liston (1776-1846) had only to appear before the footlights for an audience to break into laughter. For thirty years he commanded the London stage to become the first comic actor to earn more than a top tragedian. Liston lived at 40 Brompton Square from 1829 to 1833. One of Liston's greatest successes, playing alongside Madame Vestris (see below) was in *Sweethearts and Wives*, written in 1823 by Irish-born James Kenney (1780-1849), who spent the last three years of his life at 22 (now 20) South Terrace, Alexander Square. Kenney, who suffered from a nervous affliction, enjoyed the literary society of his day, despite repeatedly being taken for an escaped lunatic.

112. No. 22 Brompton Square in which George Colman the Younger lived and died.

William Farren (1786-1861) was born the son of an actor who bequeathed him £8,000, a sum which enabled him to forsake the boards for a successful career in management. Popular with the public, he was in private life unsocial, unintellectual and tight with money. Farren lived at 23 Brompton Square in 1824-36, moved to No. 30 from 1837 to 1853 and back to No. 23 from 1854 to 1861.

John Baldwin Buckstone (1802-79) made his debut in a barn at Peckham but by the age of twenty-five was appearing at the Adelphi in one of his own plays. Prolific as a dramatist and talented as a farceur, Buckstone's success with *Married Life* (1834) enabled him to move to 2 Onslow Terrace the following year. In 1838 Buckstone tried to place his son at the Western Grammar School in Alexander Place (*see p. 68*).

113. John Buckstone, resident of 6 Brompton Square.

His offer to buy a share as a proprietor in the enterprise was rebuffed "on the ground that I am an actor and that such a person in a public school would incite in the boys a desire to see plays, which would unsettle their minds."

By 1840 Buckstone could afford to move to 6 Brompton Square and it was while he was living there that he became manager of the Haymarket, which he made the leading playhouse in London in a tenure lasting a quarter of a century. Buckstone also toured the USA with great success, acting alongside his preferred leading lady Fanny Elizabeth Fitzwilliam (1801-54), a fine singer with a gift for playing country innocents – which did not prevent her from taking up residence with him at Brompton Square. She died there suddenly, of cholera, at the height of her powers, just a month before they were to be married. Buckstone's ghost, with its distinctive chuckling drawl, is said to haunt the Haymarket still.

RUNAWAYS AND DROPOUTS

Richard J. Smith (1786-1855), known as O. Smith, forsook the security of work as a solicitor's clerk to become a runaway. A large frame and deep voice initially condemned him to be type-cast as a devil or demon but he eventually progressed to character roles in stage adaptations of Dickens' novels. Smith lived at 1 North Terrace from 1846 to 1851. At his death he left 25 volumes of theatrical ephemera, raw materials – now in the British Museum – for a projected but never written history of the British stage.

Robert Keeley (1793-1869) turned his back on the path chosen for him, breaking an apprenticeship to join a company of strolling players. He found fame in the hugely popular stage versions of the adventures of '*Tom and Jerry*' based on the lads-about-town characters created by Pierce Egan. His developed talent, however, ranged from 'low comedy' to classic cameos, ranging from Dogberry to Sairy Gamp. Keeley's wife, Mary Ann (née Goward) (1806-99), who excelled in 'breeches' roles, enjoyed her greatest triumph in the title role in a lurid and sympathetic stage biography of the dashing underworld hero and jail-breaker *Jack Sheppard* (1839), written by John Baldwin Buckstone (see above). In 1845 the

114. Mary Ann Keeley.

115. The Keeleys' house at 10 Pelham Crescent.

Keeleys moved to 19 Brompton Square and in 1856 to 10 Pelham Crescent, where Robert died in 1869, Mary Ann outliving him there for another thirty years.

Benjamin Nottingham Webster (1797-1882) was yet another runaway who progressed via character roles in works by Boucicault (see below) and Buckstone to become simultaneously manager of the Adelphi and the Haymarket. He also wrote some one hundred plays and made his last appearance, in a benefit, at 79. From 1841 to 1854 he lived at 3 Brompton Road. Alfred Sidney Wigan (1814-78), a member of Webster's company, lived at 6 St Michael's Grove (1846-9) and 13 (now 23) Pelham Place 1849-52. Wigan, a considerable French scholar, excelled in roles requiring French or broken English. He eventually died at 33 Brompton Square.

James Robinson Planché (1796-1880), son of a watchmaker of Huguenot descent, threw up an apprenticeship to a bookseller to write for the stage, providing plays for both Webster and Buckstone and libretti for Weber and Mendelssohn and developing a long-term relationship as a favoured dramatist of Madame Vestris. Piracy of his work provoked him to campaign successfully for a Dramatic Copyright Act, extending legal protection to works written for the stage. Planché also pursued life-long interests in costume and heraldry. In 1823 he provided Kemble with historically accurate costumes for his revival of King John – a 'first' for the English stage. In 1834 he published a definitive *History of British Costume,* based on a decade of diligent study, which long remained a standard reference for historical painters. A Fellow of the Society of Antiquaries from his youth, Planché was appointed to the College of Heralds in 1854 and eventually became Somerset Herald. One of his last projects was to organize the armour collections of the Tower of London into an historically coherent display. The *Oxford Companion to the Theatre* notes acidly that "his work for the theatre, which was extremely successful in its day, seems to have had no literary merit whatever and divorced from its music and spectacular effects is quite unreadable" ... but the same authority does concede that the texts of these extravaganzas were to prove a major source of inspiration for W.S. Gilbert's libretti for the Savoy operas. Planché was the first occupant of 6 Egerton Terrace.

John Reeve (1799-1838) came to the stage by stages, forsaking the hosiery trade and Gosling's bank for amateur theatricals. Irritated by always being assigned minor parts, Reeve hired a theatre entirely on his own account to play the lead in *Othello* with a company of his own choosing. He discovered that his great gift was for mimicry, which he used to establish his reputation in a farce adapted from Colman the Younger. He also triumphed as Jerry Hawthorne in Egan's *Tom and Jerry*. The public adored him but he was a sore trial to management, constantly drunk and constantly failing to master his lines. Buckstone handled him skilfully by drafting parts which consisted of little more than catch-phrases, leaving him to fill out the role by using his competence as a dancer, singer and droll with "great flexibility of feature and limb". Reeve himself played shamelessly on the sympathy of his audience, amending each stumble with a nod or a wink or a hissed reminder that he liked his glass as much as they did. During his final season in 1837 he gave one of the first theatrical representations of Sam Weller but having once more conspicuously failed to master his part in another drama, suffered a collapse on his way home from its second performance. He died at his house at 46 Brompton Row on 24 January 1838.

PROBLEMS WITH MONEY

Dramatist Charles Dance (1794-1863), son of the distinguished architect George Dance, spent thirty years working as an official of the debtor's court while in his off hours churning out a stream of farces and burlettas, often in collaboration with J.R. Planché. Such works gained him the favour of the discerning Madame Vestris and membership of the Garrick Club.

Many other theatricals were less fortunate – or less prudent – than Dance. Alfred Bunn (1796-1860) was as famed for his literary feuds as for his simultaneous management of Drury Lane and Covent Garden. From 1835 to 1839 he lived at Eagle Lodge, Old Brompton. Despite his talent for attracting the very best talent the dual role proved too much for him and he was declared bankrupt in 1840, the year in which he published his memoirs in three volumes.

The long, eventful and interlocking careers of Charles James Mathews (1803-78) and his wife could have provided the basis for a television mini-series had the format existed in their day. Mathews was born the son of Charles Mathews (1776-1835), the gifted mimic, pioneer of one-man shows (written for him by Colman the Younger) and manager of the Adelphi. Mathews' wife has gone down in theatrical history as 'Madame Vestris' (1797-1856) but was born Lucia Elizabetta Bartolozzi. Deserted by her French ballet-dancer husband Armand Vestris in 1820, she abandoned singing for burlesque, graduating to management of the Olympic in 1830 and there presenting farces scripted for her by Planché. As a manager she made significant contributions to raising theatrical standards – improving scenery, using historically accurate costumes and real rather than fake 'props', and pioneering the 'box-set', an on-stage representation of a room, complete with ceiling. In 1835, on the death of Charles Mathews senior, his son inherited the management of the Adelphi. In the same year Mathews junior made his professional stage debut – at Mme. Vestris' Olympic – in his own play, *The Hump-backed Lover*. In 1838 Mathews and Vestris married and thereafter their careers ran in parallel. At Covent Garden they staged a fine production of *London Assurance*

116. Charles Mathews.

117. Madame Vestris.

(1841) by the nineteen-year-old Dion Boucicault. Acclamation was not, however, matched by financial success. A further term at the Lyceum proved similarly abortive. From 1848 to 1854 they had lived in some style at Gore Lodge, Brompton Park Lane, but their tenancy ended with their impending bankruptcy, followed shortly by the death of Mme. Vestris. Mathews eventually bounced back, re-establishing his career by a sojourn in New York, where he met and married Lizzie Davenport (?-1899), another actress who proved an excellent support. By 1865 they were back in London, living at 23 Pelham Crescent. Elegant and perennially improvident, Mathews managed to keep his head above water financially and continued to excel in frivolous roles reflecting his own light-hearted character.

John Palgrave Simpson (1807-87) was born in comfortable circumstances in Norwich, educated at Cambridge, declined to take holy orders and travelled in central Europe until the collapse of his father's fortune obliged him to write novels, a good account of Hungary and eyewitness descriptions of revolutionary Paris. Settling at 9 Alfred Place West (now Thurloe Street) in 1850, Simpson devoted himself assiduously to writing for the stage, turning out some sixty works in a career of thirty-three years, most successfully adaptations from French drama and Dickens.

LIVING LEGENDS

By the time Fanny Kemble (1809-93) moved into 26 Hereford Square in 1884 she was a theatrical legend, long since retired. Born into a formidable theatrical dynasty, daughter of Charles Kemble and niece of the legendary Sarah Siddons, Fanny was not intended for the boards but educated at a genteel 'academy' at 22 Hans Place, where fellow pupils included writer Laetitia Landon and Caroline Lamb, future lover of Lord Byron. At twenty, however, Fanny found herself obliged to act to save her father from bankruptcy. Her Juliet was a sensation, launching a brief but highly successful career. She left the stage in 1834 to marry a wealthy American admirer, moved to the USA, discovered that she loathed slavery – the basis of her husband's fortune –divorced him and re-launched herself on a new career, giving readings from Shakespeare. Fanny finally settled in London in 1868 and produced eight volumes of autobiography. She left Hereford Square in 1890.

118. Fanny Kemble.

Dublin-born Dionysius – 'Dion' – Boucicault (?1820-90), having acted briefly and to little effect, burst upon the metropolis, barely out of his teens, with a triumphant production of his *London Assurance*, one of the most successful of his 150 plays, starring Charles Mathews and Madame Vestris. A decade later, under his own name, he took to the boards again, enjoying acclaim on both sides of the Atlantic. The 1851 census recorded a lodger at 23 Alexander Square named Dion Page, living with an eighteen year old Spanish wife named Jessey, and describing himself as a 'gentleman and dramatic author'. Dion Page's first name and date of birth imply yet another pseudonym. In 1860 Boucicault's *Colleen Bawn*, adapted from a novel by Gerald Griffin began a run of 360 nights, enabling him to live in some style at Hereford Lodge from 1861 to 1863. During this period Boucicault managed first the Adelphi, then Astley's. In 1876 Boucicault retired to the US, dumping his wife of twenty-

119. Dion Boucicault, a caricature by Spy for Vanity Fair in 1882.

120. Ellen Terry with Jack Russells.

three years in favour of other 'nuptial arrangements'. A decade after his death the author of Boucicault's entry in the *Dictionary of National Biography* noted caustically that his "brilliant literary and histrionic qualities were not supported by any very rigorous moral code."

Ellen Terry (1847-1928) lived at 33 Longridge Road from 1878 to 1889 and from 1889 to 1902 at 22 Barkston Gardens. These were the years of her greatest fame, her departure from Barkston Gardens coinciding with the ending of her triumphant partnership with Sir Henry Irving – whose estranged wife lived a few streets away at 27 Gilston Road from 1877 until 1908. Terry made her stage debut at eight and learned her trade as part of the Keans' company. Returning to the stage in 1874 after two marriages and a long absence, Ellen Terry appeared more brilliant than ever. Having married an actor eight years her junior, in 1878 she was engaged by Henry Irving at the Lyceum. Their partnership, on and off stage, dominated the theatre for the next twenty years on both sides of the Atlantic. After the break-up of her relationship with Irving, she moved out of Barkston Gardens and took to yet another career as a theatrical manager. Her last marriage, to American actor, James Carew (really Usselman), nearly thirty years her junior, foundered after two years. As Shaw was to note wryly, "one may say that her marriages were adventures and her friendships enduring." In her later life Ellen Terry acted but little, though she gave celebrated readings from Shakespeare and lectured on his work as well.

The career of (Walter) Brandon Thomas (1856-1914) was a one hit wonder – but what a hit! *Charley's Aunt* ran for four straight years from its premiere at the tiny Royalty theatre in Soho in 1892. At one time it was running simultane-

121. *Barkstone Gardens, home of Ellen Terry from 1889 to 1902.*

122. *Brandon Thomas.*

ously in forty-eight theatres across the world and being performed in twenty-two languages, ranging from Esperanto to Gaelic, from Afrikaans to Zulu. Little wonder that Thomas could afford to move into 22 The Boltons in 1900.

THEATRICAL KNIGHTS

Like many successful literary men of his day Sir William Schwenk Gilbert (1836-1911) was initially a failed barrister. It was appropriate, therefore, that he should enjoy his first major triumph with *Trial by Jury* (1875). This initiated a twenty-year collaboration with composer Sir Arthur Sullivan, recently the organist of St Peter's, Cranley Gardens. By 1878 Gilbert could afford to move into 24 The Boltons where he stayed until 1881. In 1883 he took up residence in purpose-built, palatial splendour at 39 Harrington Gardens, a Flemish Gothic fantasy equipped with such avant-garde luxuries as central heating and a telephone link to the newly-built Savoy Theatre. It was at Harrington Gardens that Gilbert was to write *Princess Ida, The Mikado, Ruddigore, The Yeomen of the Guard* and *The Gondoliers*. He moved out in 1890 when he acquired Grimsdyke, a massive pseudo-Tudor

manor house at Harrow, where additions and alterations were made for him by Ernest George and Harold Peto, the architects of Harrington Gardens. Evidently feeling the need to retain a London base, Gilbert acquired 36 Prince's Gardens in 1894 but left it in 1898 following the failure of the last and only unsuccessful Savoy opera, *The Grand Duke*.

Sir Herbert Beerbohm Tree (1853-1917) lived at 31 Rosary Gardens from 1886 to 1888, during which period he made the transition from acting to management by taking over first the Comedy Theatre and then the Haymarket. Tree later staged Wilde's *A Woman of No Importance* (1893) and the smash hit *Trilby* (1895) in which he himself played the evil Svengali. He went on to open Her Majesty's Theatre, co- found the Royal Academy of Dramatic Art and play Professor Higgins to Mrs Patrick Campbell's Eliza Doolittle in the first English production of Shaw's *Pygmalion*.

123. William Schwenk Gilbert.

124. A room in Gilbert's house at 39 Harrington Gardens.

125. Sir Herbert Beerbohm Tree.

Ex-barrister Nigel Playfair (1874-1934), who lived at 26 Pelham Crescent from 1910 to 1922, learned acting under Beerbohm Tree and triumphed as Bottom in Granville-Barker's 1912 production of *A Midsummer Night's Dream*. In 1919 Playfair took over the management of the Lyric Theatre, Hammersmith, then a flea-pit cinema. Under Playfair the Lyric achieved distinction in presenting Restoration and eighteenth century drama. His 1920 production of Gay's *Beggar's Opera* ran for over fifteen hundred performances.

CONSUMMATE CONFORMIST

Ernest Thesiger (1879-1961), specialist in playing snooty upper-class Englishmen, was the grandson of a Lord Chancellor. Eschewing the Civil Service in favour of the Slade School of Fine Art, he became a member of a homosexual circle which included Willie Ranken and Oscar Wilde's friend Robert Ross, through whom he became an understudy at the St James's Theatre, with which Wilde had been particularly associated. Wounded in the Great War, Thesiger in 1917 married Janette, Willie Ranken's sister, moving into 6 Montpelier Terrace. The marriage was never consummated but was convenient for both parties, Janette being in love with the poet Margaret Jourdain. Ernest, outwardly conformist, delighted in shocking dinner parties by revealing green painted toe-nails and pearls worn next to his skin. He returned successfully to the stage to win Shaw's particular approval as a perfect Professor Higgins and the first Dauphin in *Saint Joan*. He also appeared in drag in the 1925 Cochran Revue and played Piers Gaveston, the king's 'favourite', in *Edward II*. In 1927 Thesiger published a volume of autobiography, archly entitled *Practically True*. Allegedly he charged fifty pounds for a mention in it – and seventy-five for omission. Thesiger lived at 8 St George's Court, Gloucester Road from 1939 until his death.

WELSH WIZARD

Emlyn Williams (1905-87) was the archetypal Welsh scholarship boy, who won a place at Christ Church, Oxford and then on graduation chose the uncertainties of repertory theatre. Initially an actor, he had his first success as a dramatist when he was just twenty-five and confirmed his reputation with two plays which became 'standards' – the grisly chiller *Night Must Fall* (1935) and *The Corn is Green* (1938), a semi-autobiographical exploration of the relationship between a young Welsh miner and his female teacher. By the time Williams was living at 15 Pelham Crescent between 1953 and 1960, he had developed a new career, giving public readings as Charles Dickens. In 1955 he switched to reading Dylan Thomas, re-enacting the poet's autobiographical account of his Swansea childhood in *A Boy Growing Up*. It was also during this period that Williams composed his own autobiography, *George*, which was published in 1961. George was his own real first name, Emlyn being his second.

A CHIP OFF THE OLD BLOCK

Douglas Fairbanks Junior (1909-2000) initially followed his famous father into the movies, despite his father's active hostility. Doug Junior swashed and buckled manfully enough to establish a solid if unspectacular career in silent movies and successfully transferred to sound. Between 1934 and 1937 he made five films in Britain and fell in love with the country. During World War Two Britain returned the compliment while Fairbanks served in the US Navy, mostly in the UK. He made his last two films in Britain, retiring from acting in 1951 to develop a diverse career

126. Alfred Hitchcock, film director, at home in Cromwell Road c.1930, with his wife Alma and his production secretary.

as a writer, producer and businessman. A confirmed Anglophile and high profile figure in London society in the 1950s Fairbanks lived in discreet opulence at No. 28 The Boltons – discreet enough, anyway, about his photographically recorded relationship with the Duchess of Argyll, which has recently been verified. In his sixties and seventies he returned to the screen in glossy cameo roles.

CARRYING ON ....

Comedienne Hattie Jacques (1924-80), well-loved stalwart of fourteen *'Carry On'* films, initially served as a factory worker and a nurse in World War Two before making her stage debut at the age of twenty and her first film two years later. By then she had moved into the property at 65 Eardley Crescent where she was to live for the rest of her life. From 1948 to 1950 she appeared in Tommy Handley's landmark radio series *ITMA*, and from 1950 to 1954 in *Educating Archie*. Her television partnership with Eric Sykes lasted from 1959 until her death.

127. A plaque on the house of comedienne, Hattie Jacques, at 65 Eardley Crescent.

BEHIND THE SCENE ....

The influence of theatrical agent Peggy Ramsay, who lived in a basement flat in Redcliffe Square, may be gauged from the fact that when she died, bequeathing her papers to the British Library, they were judged significant enough for a selection to be exhibited in its own showcase in the King's Library of the British Museum. Peggy Ramsay gained a wider, posthumous fame as the subject of *Love is Where it Falls*, actor Simon Callow's autobiographical account of their passionate but platonic relationship.

Enterprise, Endeavour and Exile

A MAN OF MANY PARTS

If the distinctive character of South Kensington can be attributed to any single person it must be Sir Henry Cole (1808-82), who worked tirelessly to create what became the Victoria and Albert Museum, as well as promoting the Royal Albert Hall and the National Training School for Music. The son of a professional soldier, Cole was educated at Christ's Hospital and at fifteen became clerk to the antiquarian Sir Francis Palgrave. Cole's artistic talents led him to study water-colour technique under one of its most distinguished practitioners, David Cox; later in life he would learn engraving and etching. As a young man Cole shared a house owned by the novelist Thomas Love Peacock, whose works in his old age Cole was to edit as a labour of love. Cole was also subsequently to become a great friend of Thackeray. Through Peacock Cole was introduced to a discussion group whose members included the philosopher John Stuart Mill and the historian of Greece, George Grote. Cole meanwhile was achieving seniority as a government archivist but still found time to play a leading role in the movement to establish a modern postal system. He also supplemented his income to support a growing family – eight children in all – by penning children's stories and writing tourist guidebooks under the pseudonym Felix Summerly. In 1843 Cole got the Royal Academician John Calcott Horsley, Brunel's brother-in-law, to design the first ever Christmas card. Cole was simply too busy to write his usual seasonal letter to friends and thought of the card as a short cut. One thousand were printed and then coloured by hand. Those not used by Cole and Horsley were sold off by the printer at the considerable price of a shilling each. The Christmas card as a general custom took another twenty years to catch on. In 1845 Cole won a competition organised by the Society of Arts for the design of a tea service, subsequently mass-produced by Minton. In 1846 he joined the Society of Arts which organised exhibitions of 'Art Manufactures' annually for the three subsequent years. In retrospect these can be seen as harbingers of the Great Exhibition of 1851 in the organisation of which Cole was to play so prominent a part, being appointed C.B. in recognition of his efforts. Cole served as Chairman of the Society of Arts in 1851 and 1852 and in the latter year was appointed secretary to the Department of Science and Art. From 1853 to 1873 he served as director of what was initially known as the South Kensington Museum. Cole lived at 24 Onslow Square in 1856-7, 17 Onslow Square 1857-63 and 33 Thurloe Square from 1873 to 1877. By 1880, describing himself as 'Civil Servant Superannuated', he had moved to 106 Philbeach Gardens and was working with the builder of the area, George Edward Mineard, to organise a 'Fifth of November Club' to provide an annual firework display in the communal garden. The two men also collaborated on developing a drainage system to prevent the escape of sewer gas, a topic on which Cole had developed a virtual obsession. In 1881 Cole moved to No. 96 where he experimented with a new type of conservatory porch and mused on a scheme to employ convicts to make street names and house numbers out of mosaic. He died there in 1882.

128. Sir Henry Cole.

THE SCIENTISTS

Benjamin Thompson (1753-1814), often better known by his continental title, Count Rumford, bought 168 Brompton Road (then 45 Brompton Row) in 1798 on returning from a decade abroad. American-born but a Loyalist, he moved to London in 1776 and made experiments with gunpowder. Knighted in 1784, he was made a count of the Holy Roman Empire for his military and welfare reforms in Bavaria. Thompson's investigations into the nature of heat were incorporated into numerous improvements in cooking and heating equipment. The Brompton property was extensively altered to reflect the owner's preoccupations with the physics of heat. The front windows were double-glazed by the addition of projecting oriel windows which doubled as propagators for seedlings. Stoves were concealed in the walls and in the kitchen the cooking equipment could be screened off when not actually in use. Upstairs the beds were convertible to sofas for daytime use. While living in Brompton Thompson founded the Royal Institution to advance the popular understanding of science through lectures and demonstrations. Thompson made only occasional use of the Brompton property after 1803 but it stayed in the ownership of his family for a generation after his death.

Sir Francis Galton (1822-1911), who lived at 42 Rutland Gate for half a century, had been born into a Quaker family affluent enough for him to abandon plans for a medical career and devote his youthful energies to sport, travel and exploration in Africa. The outcome of these exertions was a handbook, *The Art of Travel*, which stayed in print for forty years. Galton is now, however, chiefly remembered for his forty years of research into patterns of heredity, which ultimately resulted in the legacy of his personal fortune to establish a chair of eugenics at University College, London. He also made valuable contributions to statistics, experimental psychology and meteorology, coining the term 'anticyclone'. The most direct scientific benefit to come from his restless curiosity was the establishment of fingerprinting as a basic tool of forensic investigation. Galton was an active member of the Royal Geographical Society and the British Association and a Fellow of the Royal Society.

Sir Charles Tilston Bright (1832-88), who lived at 20 Bolton Gardens from 1874 to 1886, was the man responsible for laying the first submarine telegraph cable between Europe and America. Appointed chief engineer to the project at just twenty-four years of age, on its successful completion he was knighted at twenty-six. He served as a Liberal MP for Greenwich in his thirties but devoted much of his later life to technical improvements in insulation and other aspects of telegraphy and to supervising the laying of cables in the Mediterranean, the Gulf and the West Indies, hazardous work in wearing climates which undermined his health.

He served as President of the Institute of Electrical Engineers in the year before his early death.

Sir Henry Roscoe (1833-1915), having trained at Heidelberg under Bunsen, rejuvenated science teaching at Owen's College, Manchester and wrote a standard text, *Lessons in Elementary Chemistry* (1866) before becoming Vice-Chancellor of the University of London and a Liberal MP for Manchester. Roscoe's interests ranged from the chemical action of light to the treatment of sewage. He also did much to promote technical education and the professionalization of industrial chemistry and served as chairman of the 1851 scholarship committee. Roscoe lived at 10 Bramham Gardens from 1883 until 1914.

Sir Lyon Playfair, who lived at 18 Onslow Gardens and 17 Thurloe Place, was one of the first British scientists to hold major public office. Born in India of Scottish parents, he studied medicine at Glasgow and Edinburgh, before becoming a student of the great German chemist Liebig. An indefatigable committee man, Playfair was one of the organizers of the 1851 Exhibition and also sat on committees investigating public health, the Irish famine and the reform of the civil service. Playfair also served as Professor of Chemistry at the School of Mines and helped establish both the Royal College of Science and the South Kensington Museum.

Elected MP in 1868, he served as Deputy Speaker of the Commons in 1880-83 and was eventually elevated to the peerage as first Baron Playfair.

THE ARCHAEOLOGISTS

Augustus Henry Lane-Fox Pitt-Rivers (1827-1900) lived – attended by no less than eleven servants – at 19/21 Penywern Road from 1878 to 1881, years which marked a crucial turning-point in his life. A soldier by profession, Pitt-Rivers had built a successful career around a sustained campaign to raise the army's standards of musketry. In 1880 he inherited an estate of 29,000 acres in Wiltshire, an inheritance which was to prove immensely rich in remains ranging across the prehistoric, Roman and Saxon periods. Retiring from service in 1882 with the rank of lieutenant-general, Pitt-Rivers threw himself with ardour into excavating barrows, cemeteries, camps and even whole villages on his Wiltshire lands. In an age of enthusiastic amateurs, when many excavators displayed the motives and methods of mere treasure-hunters, Pitt-Rivers developed disciplined and systematic procedures based on the principles of total excavation, meticulous recording of stratigraphy and prompt publication of results. It was entirely appropriate that the 'father of British archaeology' should be appointed the nation's first official inspector of ancient monuments.

Excavating the virtually intact tomb of the pharaoh Tutankhamun in 1922 made Howard Carter (1874-1939) the most famous archaeologist in the world. Born and brought up at 10 Rich Terrace, Richmond Road (now Old Brompton Road) the son of animal painter Samuel John Carter, Howard Carter lived at 19 Collingham Gardens as an adult. He first went to Egypt at seventeen, trained briefly under Flinders Petrie and by twenty-five was inspector-in-chief of monuments in Upper Egypt and Nubia. Recording and clearing the contents of Tutankhamun's tomb took ten full seasons (1922-32) and broke Carter's health. He died, after a grievous illness, with the project still unfinished.

THE BROKEN MAN OF IRON

By the time Andrew Bonar Law (1858-1923) moved into 24 Onslow Gardens in 1921 he was expecting to retire from public life. In fact he was on the eve of becoming Prime Minister. Born in Kingston, New Brunswick, the son of an Ulster Presbyterian minister, at the age of eleven he was sent to Scotland to attend Glasgow High School. Entering a relative's bank at sixteen, he mastered French and German and went on to success as an iron merchant and director of Clydesdale Bank. Elected a Unionist MP in 1900, Bonar Law lost his post as Parliamentary Secretary to the Board of Trade in the Conservative electoral debacle of 1905. In the long run this proved to be his making. As the compromise candidate for the leadership of a party still in disarray he succeeded A.J. Balfour in 1911.

Party leadership pitched Bonar Law into the crisis propelling Ireland towards civil war. His own Ulster roots opposed him to Irish Home Rule and made him an ally of the intransigent ultra-Unionist Carson. The Great War, however, put the Irish crisis on hold, enabling Bonar Law to devote himself, as Colonial Secretary, to keeping the Dominions in the war, and then, as Chancellor, to finding ways of paying for it. At the same time he suffered the personal tragedy of losing two sons on active service.

129. Andrew Bonar Law.

In the post-war coalition Bonar Law, as Lord Privy Seal and Leader of the House, was *de facto* premier while Lloyd George was at the Paris peace conference. Early in 1921 Bonar Law's health broke down so badly that he resigned the Tory leadership. In 1922, however, the Lloyd George coalition finally shattered and Bonar Law, re-elected Tory leader as a 'safe pair of hands', finally became Prime Minister in October of that year.

Keynes thought Bonar Law ultra-cautious by instinct. Lloyd George dismissed him contemptuously as terminally indecisive. More to the point he was a burnt out case, ground down by the tensions of Ulster and strain of office, compounded by personal grief. Bonar Law presided in person over a conference of Allied premiers which failed signally to reach agreement over German war reparations. Despatching Baldwin to America to negotiate repayment terms for war loans, the ex-banker was dismayed to find himself bound to accept an unyielding schedule. But that soon ceased to be his problem. Diagnosed with incurable cancer in May 1923, he resigned and died in October. On leaving Westminster Abbey the former Liberal premier Asquith remarked with irreverent levity "it is fitting that we should have buried the Unknown Prime Minister by the side of the Unknown Warrior".

EXILES

Francois Guizot (1787-1874) was the son of a counter-revolutionary guillotined in 1794 and spent his boyhood years in Swiss exile. Professor of History at the University of Paris at the age of 25, Guizot as a rising academic star turned out multi-volume histories of Europe and of France before entering politics. As minister of education under King Louis-Philippe, hoping to inoculate his countrymen against revolution through education, he was responsible for the law of 1833 which required every French commune to establish a free primary school where a secular education would be accessible to all. Guizot's own ultra-bourgeois outlook on life was summarised in his exhortation to his countrymen "Enrich yourself by saving and work." After serving as ambassador to London and then foreign minister Guizot was forced out of office in 1848 by the crisis which brought down the monarchy and ushered in the Second Republic. Guizot fled to London and took up residence at 21 Pelham Crescent. He returned to France the following year but, failing to rally resistance to the new regime, remained politically marginalised and devoted himself to writing an even longer multi-volume history of France – up to the year 1789.

The career of Giuseppe Mazzini (1805-72) by contrast ended in disappointment rather than anticlimax. A child prodigy, he entered university at 14, practised as a poor man's lawyer, dabbled in journalism and dreamed of literary fame. Joining the Carbonari, an anti-absolutist secret society, he was betrayed, imprisoned and sent into exile. In Marseilles in 1832 Mazzini founded the secret revolutionary society Young Italy to free the peninsula from foreign and absolutist rule and unite it as a republic. As an insurrectionary organisation Young Italy proved a disastrous failure and by 1837 Mazzini was in exile in London where he started a school for Italian boys and published a populist newspaper. Returning to Italy during the revolution of 1848, he served briefly under Garibaldi before coming back to London in disgust at the monarchist tendency of the emerging unification movement. In 1849 he returned to Italy again to head the short-lived Roman republic. In 1851, back in London once more, he founded the Friends of Italy and plotted further abortive uprisings. Another brief period of service under Garibaldi in 1860, was followed by a final return to London and a decade of residence at 2 Onslow Terrace (subsequently 18 Fulham Road, now covered by St George's Court, Brompton Road). Here he fantasized about seizing Rome or Venice. In 1870 he left London for the last time to head yet another abortive republican rising in Sicily, where he was much admired. Italy was finally united in that year – as a monarchy.

130 Guiseppe Mazzini.

Confined to Barracks

SERVANTS OF EMPIRE

Britain's empire and its seemingly relentless expansion provided an immense diversity of career opportunities and challenges for valorous youths who were still children when Napoleon was being defeated and bundled off into exile. Half a century later dozens of them were to be found residing in the Brompton area. Many, having developed scholarly or technical interests, doubtless found the proximity of the museums and learned societies of the area congenial; others, probably, were simply attracted by the recommendations of brother officers or the prospect of clubbable neighbours. The adventurous and varied lives of these servants of empire illustrate how – in the absence of colleges of 'management education' and at a time when the ancient universities were largely indifferent to technology and generally contemptuous of non-European cultures – personnel of the armed services and East India Company frequently transcended narrow military preoccupations to contribute significantly to many other aspects of Britain's national life.

17 Rich Col. Frederick Henry, R.E.
19 Nesbett John More
21 Gabrielli Mrs.
23 Johnston Chas. Edwd.
25 Smith Duncan Adam
27 Symons Simon
29 Parr Col. Henry Hallam, C.M.G.
31 Langley Capt. Henry
33 Lambert Mrs.
35 Partridge Fredk. John
SOUTH KENSINGTON HOTEL, James Bailey
NORTH SIDE.
2 Amphlett Edward Greenfield
4 Butler Miss
6 Durant Charles
8 Brinton Roland Danvers, M.D., physician
10 Maddy Edwin Davis
12 Barry Capt. Alexander Robert Hume
16 Smith Admiral Bowden, R.N.
18 Dysart Countess of
20 Massingberd Mrs. Chas. Langton
24 Law Mrs.

132. The mix of residents in Queen's Gate Terrace in 1877 includes a good quota of military men.

131. Queen's Gate Terrace c.1905.

INDIA

Britain's control of India advanced significantly during the Napoleonic years and by 1805, the year in which the East India Company established its own training college, it had become the paramount power in the sub-continent. In 1813 the Company lost its monopoly of the region's trade and henceforth increasingly resembled a state rather than a corporation. In the 1820s Assam and lower Burma were added to the sphere of British authority in the east, in the 1840s Sind and Punjab in the west. New territories brought new responsibilities, new skills and expanding opportunities for promotion and distinction.

The career of J.C. Marshman (1794-1877) was unusual in developing largely outside the framework of British rule at Serampore (Shrirampur), a Danish settlement not acquired by the British until 1845. That – and the fact that he clearly liked Indians and thought they had a right to be educated – may well account for the treatment Marshman received in his homeland when he finally retired to Redcliffe Square North in 1852. From the age of eighteen he had supported the efforts of his missionary father, functioning for the next two decades as a sort of secular bishop by fund-raising for, and co-ordinating the activities of, a range of missionising enterprises. He subsequently established India's first paper-mill, its first English magazine, the *Friend of India*, an outspoken Bengali-language newspaper and a college for native education, into which he poured most of his personal fortune. He also compiled a civil law text, wrote the first history of Bengal and pursued scholarly interests in Chinese, Persian and Sanskrit. Following his return to England his attempts to place his expertise at the service of government were rebuffed and he devoted himself to completing a *History of India* which was widely praised.

The career of Daniel Eliott (1798-1872) was by contrast, unspectacular but steady and distinguished. Based on his mastery of the Tamil and Marathi languages and his contribution to devising India's legal code, it culminated in a knighthood and retirement to a handsome residence in The Boltons, where he died.

Major-General Sir Andrew Waugh (1810-78), who claimed descent from a standard-bearer at the battle of Flodden, proved to be a technical officer of matchless brilliance. Having completed the East India Company military college course in half the usual time he passed out top of his class and was Surveyor-General of India at the astonishingly young age of thirty-three. A sometime resident of 49 Gloucester Road, he became a prominent member of the Royal Geographical Society and finally died at 7 Petersham Terrace, Queen's Gate.

W.H. Morley (1815-60) served India without ever actually going there. A barrister by training, he compiled and published a valuable digest of cases decided by the Supreme Courts of India. His true bent, however, was for scholarship. A stalwart of the Royal Asiatic Society, he eventually became its librarian, as well as making valuable contributions to numismatics and the translation of Arabic and Persian manuscripts. Morley died at his home at 35 Brompton Square.

The career of John Laird Mair Lawrence (1811-79) got off to a distinctly unpromising start. At his first school he was flogged every single day – except for one day when he was flogged twice. At his second school he acquired only a taste for history. At the East India college, Haileybury, he won a prize for his mastery of Bengali but was otherwise unremarkable. Thereafter he followed his three elder brothers to an appointment in India, though as a civilian rather than in the military. There he struck his colleagues as unremarkable in ability and charmless in manner. He nevertheless set himself to master Hindi and Persian and, after transfer to an administrative post in Delhi, began to work hard and to enjoy the work. A decade later Lawrence was ordered home to recover his health. Returning in 1843, he finally distinguished himself by hastily improvising a huge supply train which enabled the governor-general, Lord Hardinge, to follow up his defeat of the Sikhs with a second victory. Having made himself similarly useful during the second Sikh war, Lawrence became the pacifier of newly-conquered Punjab, a territory the size of France, organising the provision of coinage, canals, roads and irrigation, securing a fair administration of justice and taxation and suppressing banditry. Lawrence believed, then and throughout his career, that the best security for British rule lay in a contented peasantry and in local elites reconciled to British suzerainty by just dealing and respect for local tradition. Adventures beyond the frontiers of British India he judged to be at best a meddling waste of resources, better spent elsewhere on the positive development of agriculture and communications, at worst as dangerous provocations likely to prove hugely counter-productive in loss of lives and treasure.

Notwithstanding Lawrence's by now acknowledged ability to confer with local people in their own language and on their own terms, the great rebellion of 1857 was as much a shock to him as to any. Despite this – and his civilian standing – he swiftly resumed the quasi-military role he had played in the Sikh wars, acting as a *de facto* general in raising supplies and loyal troops to re-take rebellious Delhi from the by now secure base of Punjab. In 1858 Lawrence returned to England to be honoured by the City of London and the universities of Oxford and Cambridge, elevated to a baronetcy and sworn of the Privy Council.

After five years of semi-retirement as, in effect, a government consultant on Indian affairs, Lawrence returned to India as viceroy. In office his curbs on official extravagance provoked unpopularity with his subordinates, while his concern to extend the steady but undramatic improvement of irrigation and railways won little credit from superiors. Retiring after a full five-year term Lawrence took up residence at 26 Queen's Gate and threw himself into the work of the newly created London School Board, of which he soon became a dedicated chairman.

At his death Lawrence was honoured with burial in Westminster Abbey. His statue still stands in Waterloo Place.

GLOBETROTTERS

Aristocratic by descent and autocratic by temperament, Admiral Robert Fitzroy (1805-65) commanded *HMS Beagle* on its epoch-making circumnavigation (1831-6) with the young naturalist Charles Darwin, served as governor of New Zealand (1843-5), where he outraged the settlers by his open sympathy for the Maoris, and then, after a short spell as commandant of the Woolwich dockyard, commanded the appropriately named screw-frigate *Arrogant*. Retiring from active service in 1850, Fitzroy was elected F.R.S. the following year, having already been awarded

133. The headquarters of the Royal Geographical Society – Lowther Lodge in Kensington Gore, designed by R. Norman Shaw, architect of Albert Hall Mansions. It became the haunt of many retired military men.

the Gold Medal of the Royal Geographical Society for his work in surveying the southern hemisphere. Appointed to head the newly established Meteorological Office, where he instituted a system of storm warnings which eventually developed into today's daily weather forecast, Fitzroy also served as secretary of the Lifeboat Association. His self-imposed labours eventually proved too much and he committed suicide, having lived at 38 Onslow Square from 1854 until the time of his death.

Sir Henry Barkly (1815-98) proved gifted as a conciliator of settler interests and smoother of ruffled feathers in colonial legislatures. An MP at thirty, he was governor of British Guiana at thirty-three and then successively governor of Jamaica, Victoria, Mauritius and Cape Colony. An enthusiastic promoter of railways and, less happily, of coolie labour, he retired in 1877 to devote his energies to the Royal Society and Royal Geographical Society, being a Fellow of both, and to the London Library, of which he was an active committee member. He died at 1 Bina Gardens.

Major-General Sir John Lefroy (1817-90), son of a rector and a gunner by training, was a fervent Christian by conviction, an antiquarian by avocation and by opportunity a tireless recorder of magnetic and meteorological observations, from St Helena to the Canadian Arctic. These interests were honoured by his elevation to Fellowships of the Society of Antiquaries and the Royal Geographical Society. In the course of a wide-ranging career Lefroy championed the medical reforms of Florence Nightingale, founded the school of gunnery at Shoeburyness, the Royal Artillery Institute and the Canadian Institute, wrote a textbook on artillery which served as the standard work for thirty years, became chief army adviser on inventions and supervised the reform of army education. When residing at 82 Queen's Gate in 1871 he had but recently retired from the army as director-general of ordnance. During an equally energetic and productive second career he served as Governor of Bermuda and Tasmania, contributing vigorously and imaginatively to the scientific and cultural life of both colonies.

The career of Sir Edmund Henderson (1821-96) was remarkable as much for its variety as its eminence. An engineer by training, his first professional task was to demarcate the border of New Brunswick, his next to organise a new convict settlement in Western Australia. Returning home, Henderson left the army to implement a wide-ranging programme of reform in the civilian prison system. In 1869 he took up the post of Chief Commissioner of the Metropolitan Police. During his tenure of office the strength of the force rose from 9,000 to 13,000 and a Criminal Investigation Department of 215 detectives was at last formally established. The provision of shelters for London's cabmen was but one among the many philanthropic causes in which Henderson interested himself, his commitment being so outstanding that on his retirement the cabbies raised £1,000 to present him with a specially commissioned memento in solid silver. A gifted raconteur and talented watercolourist, Henderson throughout his career found himself promoted over men who might have resented his authority but he invariably won their respect by a combination of tact and talent. He died at 4 Gledhow Gardens.

134. The most famous soldier in Brompton was Robert Baden-Powell, who lived at 32 Princes Gate soon after his legendary defence of Mafeking, at a time when he was formulating his plans for what became the Boy Scout movement. The Scout Association is located today in Baden-Powell House in Queen's Gate.

LATE VICTORIANS

The life of Frederick Lugard (1858-1945) was as remarkable for his youthful adventures as for his mature achievements as one of the most creative of imperial proconsuls. As an officer in the Indian army he won a reputation as a fearless hunter of big game. Service in the Sudan and Burma gained him four mentions in despatches and a D.S.O. It was thanks largely to Lugard's energy and enterprise that Uganda was saved from sectarian civil war in 1890-92 and subsequently taken under British rule. And it was Lugard who, in Nigeria between 1900 and 1907, established the West African Frontier Force and crushed the military power of the Fulani emirates. A five-year stint as governor of Hong Kong was followed by a return to Nigeria as supreme governor of Britain's largest single colonial territory, which he was charged to integrate into a single administration. During these years (1912-19) Lugard maintained a London base at 51 Rutland Gate. His subsequent career involved service with the League of Nations and campaigns against slavery and for the study of African languages and cultures. Elevated to the peerage in 1928, Lugard also received five honorary degrees and the Gold Medal of the Royal Geographical Society.

Field Marshal Edmund Allenby (1861-1936), was the last great cavalry commander in the history of the British army. Born into the Nottinghamshire gentry, he was educated for imperial service at Haileybury and Sandhurst and took a commission in the Inniskillings. Service in Africa was followed by the opportunity to command in the Boer war, where he showed himself more than competent.

During the opening phase of the Great War Allenby led the First Cavalry Division in the retreat from Mons and was a commander in the first battle of Ypres. In 1917 he was promoted to command Third Army in the battle of Arras – and lost his only son in action that same year. Transferred to command the Egyptian Expeditionary Force, Allenby utilised the unsuspected military genius of T.E. Lawrence to raise a 'revolt in the desert' while himself commanding a more conventional campaign for the reconquest of Palestine, the last in which cavalry were to be used *en masse*. In the course of this enterprise Allenby captured Jerusalem, Damascus and Aleppo and annihilated a Turkish army in an historic confrontation of mounted forces at Megiddo.

After the war Allenby served as Special High Commissioner for Egypt, persuading the British government to abolish its protectorate and accept Egypt as a *de jure*, if not *de facto*, independent state. Resigning in 1925, Allenby in 1928 took up residence at 24 Wetherby Gardens. He passed his last years pursuing his passions for angling and bird-watching, building an aviary in the back garden of his London home.

George Howson (1886-1936), a trained engineer, initially worked as a rubber planter in north Borneo until invalided home on sick leave on the eve of the Great War. Wartime service brought him the rank of major, a Military Cross and a lifelong commitment to those disabled by combat. The first poppy appeal, in 1921, relied on supplies made in France by the families of *poilus* killed in action. It was Howson who seized the initiative in establishing a Royal British Legion poppy factory to create a domestic source of supply. Starting with just five disabled ex-servicemen, within three months he was employing forty and paying full male wages in an industry which had traditionally depended on the exploitation of young girls at sweatshop rates. His health, however, never really recovered from his early experience in Borneo and he died, of pancreatic cancer, aged just fifty, at his home, 5 The Boltons.

135. Another organisation to help ex-soldiers after the First World War was Lord Roberts' Workshop in which soldiers made items for sale to the public. Pictured here is the Princess Royal, with Princess Margaret, in the workshop showrooms at 122 Brompton Road c.1960

Living off Letters

SHAKESPEAREAN SHYSTER

John Payne Collier (1789-1883) was the sort of scholar who gets scholarship a bad name. Nowadays his nefarious exploits would be attributed to an attention-seeking personality disorder but in a plainer-speaking age he was simply denounced as a fraud. It was in 1840, while living at 22 Brompton Square, that Collier founded the Shakespeare Society, with himself as its first director. Payne had established his scholarly credentials in 1831 with the publication of *The History of English Dramatic Poetry to the Time of Shakespeare: and Annals of the Stage to the Restoration*. The work was dedicated to the Lord Chamberlain, then the Duke of Devonshire, who had official responsibility for stage censorship. On the strength of his *magnum opus* Payne was appointed the Lord Chamberlain's literary adviser. The *History*, while containing valuable new documentary information, was, however, tainted throughout with Collier's own fabrications. His official posts thereafter enabled him to gain access to many rare documents, on which he based further researches – and forgeries. Notable among these were his false marginal 'corrections' to a 1632 version of Shakespeare's plays, named the Perkins Folio after its supposed original annotator. Collier was exposed in 1859 but denied all. Definitive proof that he falsified not only manuscripts in private collections but even State Papers as well was found after his death in his own personal archive.

WANDERING SPIRIT

The odyssey that brought George Borrow (1803-81) to respectable retirement in Hereford Square was a long and tortuous one. Born in Norfolk the son of an army recruiting officer, Borrow had a nomadic childhood but showed early evidence of linguistic talent. He toiled as a solicitor's clerk for five years before breaking out by using his forensic confinement as the springboard for a literary career, publishing six volumes of *Celebrated Trials and Remarkable Cases of Criminal Jurisprudence*. In 1824 Borrow began wandering through rural England, making his first contact with gypsy life. Capitalising on his facility for languages, Borrow then became an

136. George Borrow; painting by his brother, John Borrow, 1821.

137. George Borrow's house in Hereford Square. Drawing by Frederick Adcock.

agent for the Bible Society, travelling through France, Germany, Russia, Portugal, Spain, Morocco and the Balkans. Periodically he fell victim to bouts of manic depression – as one might when trying to promote Protestant Bibles in countries profoundly attached to the Roman and Orthodox faiths or to Islam. Salvation came in the form of a well-to-do widow whose fortune enabled him to settle in Suffolk and devote himself to literature. Borrow's experiences in Spain issued in print as *The Zincali, or an Account of the Gypsies of Spain* (1840) and *The Bible in Spain* (1843). The latter proved an "instantaneous and overwhelming" success, blending autobiography and imagination to paint a vivid, largely truthful, picture of a land tormented by banditry and civil wars. *Lavengro* (1851) was based partly on the nomadic wanderings of his family when he was a child and partly on his experiences among gypsies. The latter provided the main focus for its sequel *The Romany Rye* (1857). Borrow moved to Hereford Square in 1860 and lived there until 1872. His later works included *Wild Wales* (1862) and *Romano Lavo-Lil, or 'Word Book of the English Gypsy Language'*. Borrow may frequently have exaggerated his linguistic prowess (among many other things) but he was among the first to take a scholarly interest in the Romany language and culture and has been hailed by the *Encyclopaedia Britannica* with perhaps calculated ambiguity as "one of the most imaginative prose writers of the nineteenth century."

BIOGRAPHER OF THE NATION

Sir Leslie Stephen (1832-1904) Etonian, Evangelical and expert on eighteenth-century English literature, was also a keen oarsman and mountaineer and thus the epitome of muscular Christianity – until he became an agnostic and abandoned his priesthood in 1870. Stephen had come to London and a literary livelihood in 1864, helping to found the *Pall Mall Gazette,* a combination of evening paper and literary review, the following year. Its name was taken from Thackeray's novel *Pendennis,* in which Captain Shandon, imprisoned in the Marshalsea prison for debt, drafts a prospectus for a periodical 'written by gentlemen for gentlemen". While living at 16 Onslow Gardens from 1867 to 1873 Stephen edited the *Alpine Journal* and in 1871 published a collection of Alpine essays as *The Playground of Europe.* In the same year he followed in the footsteps of Thackeray by accepting the editorship of the *Cornhill Magazine.* (Stephen's first wife, Minny, was Thackeray's daughter; she died in 1875). Despite Stephen's own prodigious literary output he is more widely remembered as the editorial master-mind behind the monumental *Dictionary of National Biography* (to which he personally contributed almost four hundred entries) and as the father of Virginia Woolf.

138. Sir Leslie Stephen; oil painting by George Frederick Watts.

IRISH EXILES

The life of John Banim (1798-1842) was one of talent blighted by misfortune. A prospering drawing-master, the death of his first love all but unhinged his mind until he buried his grief in poetry. Urged by friends, he moved to London, where in 1821 a triumphant production of his *Damon and Pythias,* starring Macready and Kemble, enabled him to pay off debts and move to 13 Brompton Lower Grove, where he lived from 1822 to 1824. Inspired by the success of Scott's Waverley novels, he, in collaboration with elder brother Michael (1796-1874), aspired to do for Irish genre writing what Scott had done for the speech and traditions of Scotland. *Tales by the O'Hara Family* appeared to critical and popular acclaim from 1825 onwards but Banim was already broken in health by a spinal disorder. In 1835 he returned to Kilkenny to die, receiving en route generous sums from admirers. While living at Brompton Lower Grove Banim gave his younger countryman Gerald Griffin (1803-40) lodgings there and introduced him to the *Literary Gazette*, to which both contributed. Banim also persuaded Griffin to abandon writing musical numbers in favour of fiction. The outcome was an impressive social novel *The Collegians* (1829). Despite its success Griffin then abandoned literature for the law, then gave that up to join the Christian Brothers as a teacher in Ireland before also dying, not yet forty. Twenty years later Dion Boucicault turned *The Collegians* into a hugely successful stage play *The Colleen Bawn*, a film version of which in due course became one of the earliest productions of the independent Irish cinema.

THE JOURNALISTS

Douglas Jerrold (1803-57), a successful dramatist at fifteen, had already by then been an actor, a printer and a sailor. Turning out plays for the next twenty years, he also turned increasingly, first to journalism, then to editing, becoming the editor of *Lloyd's Illustrated Weekly Newspaper*. A major contributor to *Punch* magazine until his death, Jerrold was a close friend of both Dickens and Thackeray. Jerrold lived at 46 Seymour Walk (then 6 Seymour Terrace) from 1832 to 1834, then moved to 11 Thistle Grove (now demolished and covered by Drayton Gardens) where he lived until 1836.

Sir William Howard Russell (1820-1907) virtually invented the role of foreign – and more particularly war-correspondent. Irish-born, he left Trinity College, Dublin without a degree and came to London to study law, maintaining himself by teaching maths at Kensington Grammar School. The great Delane recruited him for *The Times*, despatching him to the Crimea, where Russell's unsparing exposures of military incompetence helped bring down Lord Aberdeen's government and inspire the epoch-making mission of Florence Nightingale. It was while covering the bloody battle of Balaclava that Russell gave an immortal phrase to the English language, referring to British infantry as "the thin red line". Russell, who also covered campaigns in America, Austria, Africa and India, regarded detachment as no part of his professional obligation, writing rather with ferocious passion, whether moved by pity or by indignation. Honoured by the governments of France, Prussia,

139. Douglas Jerrold, whose house in Thistle Grove is now covered by Drayton Gardens.

140. William Howard Russell; cartoon by Ape for Vanity Fair, 1875.

141. *George Augustus Sala; caricature by Ape for Vanity Fair in 1875.*

Austria, Turkey, Greece and Portugal, he was renowned as excellent company in comfort or adversity. A lifelong friend of Edward VII, whom he accompanied on his travels, Russell also enjoyed the acquaintance of literary men. Thackeray declared he would gladly pay a guinea a day just to dine at the same table with him. Despite the many hazards of his chosen profession Russell died peacefully at his home at 202 Cromwell Road, aged eighty-seven.

George Augustus Henry Sala (1828-1895), a Londoner of Italian parentage and Parisian education, began as a book illustrator but moved swiftly on to journalism and at the age of twenty was editor of *Chat.* In 1860 he founded *Temple Bar,* which he edited until 1866. Sala, however, was anything but a desk man. He reported the Crimea for Dickens' *Household Words* and the American civil war for the *Daily Telegraph.* He was with Garibaldi in Italy and covered the Franco-Prussian war of 1870-71. In 1876 he was in Russia, in 1885 in Australia. Sala became a celebrated Fleet Street 'character', noted for his frock coat, immaculately starched white waistcoat and bulbous, rubicund nose. In 1892 he unwisely sought to capitalise on his name to establish *Sala's Journal.* It failed disastrously – with disastrous consequences. Sala was obliged to sell off most of his library to fend off creditors. Lord Rosebery arranged for a Civil List pension of £100 a year but the impoverished Sala died before he could draw it. His autobiography, published in the year of his death was appropriately entitled *Life and Adventures.* No. 1 Alexander Square was one of Sala's numerous London addresses.

THE HISTORIANS

At Oxford J.A. Froude (1818-94) fell under the charismatic spell of John Henry Newman, who famously abjured the Church of England for Rome in 1845. Froude in consequence experienced a complete spiritual crisis, which, compounded with sexual frustration, found its ca-

142. *J.A. Froude, historian and resident of 5 Onslow Gardens.*

tharsis in a dire but dramatic novel, *The Nemesis of Faith*. Its publication cost Froude his Fellowship, forcing him to forsake Oxford for London, though not to forsake scholarship entirely for journalism, vowing "I am going to stick to the History ... and I believe I shall make something of it." Writing and reviewing for periodicals led eventually to the editorship of *Fraser's Magazine* (1860 -74). The journal had declined in influence but still numbered among its contributors both Thackeray and Carlyle, a close friend, whose literary executor he became. Considering Froude's unrelenting burden of journalism and editorship, it is all the more remarkable that he should have produced a twelve-volume *History of England from the Death of Cardinal Wolsey to the defeat of the Spanish Armada*, based on close, systematic use of archives. The *Oxford Companion to English Literature* still hails it as "a distinguished work of scholarship on which all subsequent Tudor studies rest."

Froude established a national cult celebrating the daring deeds of Elizabethan sea-dogs but was criticized for being less than impartial about the English Reformation. He also wrote well and sold well on a wide range of other topics – John Bunyan, the Templars and Lord Beaconsfield. Even his ephemera were reprinted as *Short Studies in Great Subjects*. The dons were unforgiving. Froude's desertion of academia for a wider readership made him vulnerable to scholarly spite. His scholarship was impugned (quite unjustly) by E.A. Freeman, an historian whom posterity has dismissed as a boor, xenophobe and anti-Semite. As prolific as Froude, Freeman relied entirely on secondary sources. His scholarly deficiencies were to be humiliatingly exposed by the very primary sources Froude relied so closely upon. Froude did, however, give ammunition to his enemies by producing a history of eighteenth-century Ireland which was decidedly below par and was accordingly pilloried by his near neighbour, W.H. Lecky. In 1892 Lord Salisbury offered Froude the Regius Professorship of Modern History at Oxford. Returning to his *alma mater*, that year Froude vacated 5 Onslow Gardens, his home since 1865. Although the appointment met with a decidedly mixed reception, Froude, immediately proved that he could lecture as superbly as he wrote.

The true intellectual monument to Lord Acton (1834-1902) is the magisterial multi-volume *Cambridge Modern History* (1899-1912), which he planned; but he is most frequently remembered for a single, much-quoted, invariably misquoted, dictum – correctly "Power tends to corrupt and absolute power corrupts absolutely." The following sentence remains less well known but, in view of Carlyle's worship of the Hero as the moving force in history, deserves wider currency – "Great men are almost always bad men." John Emerich Edward Dahlberg Acton came of an old-established Shropshire Catholic family but his mother was a German aristocrat and he was actually born in Naples. When Acton was three his father died and his mother married wealthy, urbane Lord Granville. Acton was accordingly educated in Paris and Edinburgh and studied in Munich and Italy. At twenty-seven he was elected Whig MP for Carlow and served for six years, winning the admiration and friendship of Gladstone. He was created first Baron Acton in 1869.

From 1859 to 1864 Acton edited *The Rambler*, a Catholic monthly, resigning in response to ecclesiastical pressures on its independence. Thereafter he contributed prolifically to heavyweight periodicals like the *Quarterly Review* and the *English Historical Review*, which he helped to found and of which he became editor in 1886. Acton remained a devoted but by no means uncritical Catholic, opposing, for example, the declaration of the papal doctrine of infallibility. His declared life project was, very appropriately, nothing less than a history of liberty. It was never to be completed, though its principles were sketched in two lectures delivered in 1877, on freedom in antiquity and in Christianity respectively. It was in that same year that Acton moved into 72 Exhibition Road, where he lived until 1890.

W.H. Lecky (1838-1903), who lived at 38 Onslow Gardens from 1874 to 1903, was born and educated in Dublin and published, at the age of twenty-seven, a *History of the Rise and Influence of the Spirit of Rationalism in Europe* which made him famous. He subsequently developed his concern with the relationship between morality and theology in a *History of European Morals from Augustus to Charlemagne*. Lecky's monumental – eight volumes later extended to twelve – *History of England in the Eighteenth Century* was, in line with his previous interests, primarily devoted to political ideas, though the latter volumes concentrated on the history of Ireland, primarily with a view to refuting Froude. From 1895 to 1902 Lecky served as MP for Trinity College, Dublin.

THE POETS

Edward John Trelawny (1792-1881) wasn't exactly a poet himself but he did know some rather well. Poorly educated, sent to sea at thirteen, divorced by thirty, he used a modest private income to fund a European odyssey, during which he met, and was disappointed by, Byron but in Shelley found his *alter ego*. When Shelley drowned off Viareggio, it was Trelawny who cremated the body – which was only fair as he had designed the boat responsible. In 1823 Trelawny followed Byron to fight in the Greek war of independence and married the thirteen-year-old half-sister of a Greek revolutionary. In 1831 he published the autobiographical *Adventures of a Younger Son*, in which his exploits lost nothing in the telling. During that decade he was living in Egerton Place. In 1858 he published the slightly more trustworthy *Recollections of the Last Days of Byron and Shelley*, for which he is chiefly remembered. Trelawny's ashes were eventually buried next to those of Shelley, whose mythic status he had done so much to perpetuate. Trelawny lived at 7 Pelham Crescent from 1861 until the year of his death.

F.T. Palgrave (1824-97) who lived at 16 Cranley Place and eventually became Professor of Poetry at Oxford (1885-95) is remembered not at all for his own dozen volumes of verse but as the editor of *The Golden Treasury of best songs and Lyrical poems in the English Language* (1861) which acquired the status of a revered institution in British classrooms. Compiled with the advice of Palgrave's close friend Tennyson, it strongly reflected contemporary taste, thus omitting such major figures as Donne and Blake. A second edition appeared in the year of Palgrave's death, a fifth major revision in 1964.

Sir Edwin Arnold (1832-1904) lived at 2 Templeton Place between 1880 and 1884 and from 1898 at 31 Bolton Gardens, where he died in 1904. Arnold won the Newdigate Prize for English verse at Oxford and was appointed principal of Poona College, Bombay when only twenty-four. Returning to England in 1861, he joined the staff of the *Daily Telegraph*, becoming its editor in 1873. He published both his own poems and translations, including works from Sanskrit. His best known composition *The Light of Asia, or the Great Renunciation* (1879) runs to eight books in blank verse, tracing the life of Gautama Siddharta, founder of Buddhism, and explaining its teachings through "the medium of an imaginary Buddhist votary". It was while studying law in London (1889-91) that Gandhi first read that core text of Hindu scripture, the *Bhagavadgita* – in Arnold's English translation – and thus began his own spiritual odyssey.

143. Sir Edwin Arnold; photograph by Elliott & Fry.

Henry Austin Dobson (1840-1921) began as a poet and ended as a biographer and doyen of eighteenth-century studies. A civil servant for forty-five years, he was barely conscientious in his official capacity, reserving his energies for writing. His first volumes were published while he was living at 10 Redcliffe Street between 1873 and 1880 – a volume of light verse *Vignettes in Rhyme* (1873), *The Civil Service Handbook of English Literature* (1874), *Proverbs in Porcelain* (1877) and a biography of Hogarth (1879).

Stephane Mallarmé (1842-98) lived at 6 Brompton Square from 1862 to 1864, perfecting his English. This prosaic investment enabled him to earn a living as a language teacher at various *lycées* on his return to Paris and also to translate the work of Edgar Allan Poe into French. Mallarmé's own introspective and highly-wrought poems stand in striking contrast to the facile versification of William Morris and Lord Tennyson, which dominated English taste when he first began to publish in the 1860s. His *L'Apres-midi d'un faune* (1865) inspired Debussy's prelude of the same title. Mallarmé's *oeuvre* became characterised by an apparent clarity of language coupled with an opacity of meaning and throughout his subsequent career he continued to make increasing demands on his readers. Mallarmé acquired cult status as the master of the French symbolist movement and has been subsequently hailed as a founder of modern European poetry and forerunner of structuralism, numbering Proust, Gide and Verlaine among his personal disciples.

John Gray (1866-1934) lived at 11 Egerton Gardens from 1898 to 1905. Oscar Wilde had encouraged (indeed, paid for) the publication of Gray's first volume of verse *Silverpoints* (1893), which included translations from Mallarmé. A Nonconformist by birth, Gray converted to Roman Catholicism and was ordained in 1901. He spent many years as rector of St Peter's, Edinburgh. He was almost certainly the inspiration for Wilde's most celebrated fictional creation, the central character of *A Portrait of Dorian Gray*.

T.S. Eliot (1888-1965) lived briefly in a boarding-house at at 33 Courtfield Road in 1933 after separating from his first wife Vivien. It was a melancholy experience and Eliot was glad to accept the hospitality of Father Cheetham, vicar of St Stephen's, Gloucester Road where Eliot was to serve as churchwarden from 1934 to 1959. Although he claimed to dislike Kensington he remained in the area for seven years, living at 9 Grenville Place and 11 Emperor's Gate. It was during this period that he wrote *Murder in the Cathedral* (1935) and *Old Possum's Book of Practical Cats* (1939).

144. Beatrix Potter at the age of twenty-six.

A NATIONAL TREASURE

Beatrix Potter (1866-1943) was born at 2 The Boltons and continued to live there until her marriage in 1913. As her wealthy family considered schools vulgar Beatrix grew up a virtual recluse and compensated for her lack of playmates by absorbing herself in natural history. She also invented a cypher so fiendish that the half a million words she wrote in it were not decrypted until the 1960s. Although she had a pet hedgehog called Tiggy, undoubtedly the model for Mrs Tiggywinkle, her relationship with pets was more forensic than sentimental and she was not averse to killing and dissecting them to study their anatomy. As a teenager she passed days in the Museum of Natural History, painting expert water-colours. At eighteen she produced a publishable paper on the reproductive process of lichens but was barred from reading it before the Linnaean Society on the grounds of no academic standing and being female to boot. *The Tale of Peter Rabbit* began in 1893 as a letter to the son of her former governess. In 1901 she published it in book form at her own expense. *The Tailor of Gloucester* followed in 1902. Publisher Frederick Warne saw her potential and in 1903 made *Squirrel Nutkin* her first major success. By 1905 she was able to buy a farm at Sawtrey in the Lake District, where she had passed many childhood holidays. The farm provided the setting for another six of her books. Following her marriage to Lakeland solicitor William Heelis, Beatrix abandoned Kensington to become absorbed in sheep-breeding and buying up tracts of her adoptive home which were eventually passed over to the National Trust.

145. Panoramic view of Brompton Cemetery, 1840.

Permanent Residents

Early nineteenth-century London faced an unacknowledged burials crisis which the cholera outbreak of 1831-2 finally made it impossible to ignore. Parliament's novel solution was to supplement traditional ecclesiastical provision by authorizing the development of six cemeteries as commercial ventures. In 1837 the West London and Westminster Cemetery Company was established by 'projector' Stephen Geary, architect of a similar, more happily-fated enterprise at Highgate in north London. The Parliamentary Bill for the venture was sponsored by reforming MP Thomas Wakley, editor of *The Lancet*, then a crusading journal dedicated to the exposure of medical quackery and incompetence. Despite this seemingly auspicious provenance the progress of the undertaking was almost immediately blocked by doubts, arising from a recent entail settlement, about Lord Kensington's rights to dispose of the site selected for the cemetery. The position was not satisfactorily resolved until August 1839. An additional small strip of land, required for the road frontage on the southern side, was not acquired from the Equitable Gas Company until 1843. The Gas Company, having decided that it did not actually need the land in question, had tried to be anything but equitable and asked such an extortionate price for it that the cemetery company had rejected it outright. Happily Robert Gunter (*see p. 42*), who not only invested in the cemetery venture but also had a family mausoleum there, was able to acquire the land cheaply afterwards and sold it on to the cemetery at cost.

The architectural competition to design Brompton Cemetery, its lay-out, chapels, catacombs etc. was won, not by Geary, as might perhaps have been expected, given his leading role in the enterprise, but by the relatively unknown Benjamin A. Baud, who had served as an assistant to Sir Jeffrey Wyattville on the project to 'Gothicize' Windsor Castle. The cemetery was to be Baud's only major solo project. On the question of planting, the company engaged as its consultant the distinguished garden-designer and horticultural journalist J.C. Loudon (1783-1843), as editor of the *Gardening Magazine* probably the most eminent authority in the land.

By 1840 the walls had been built, avenues of lime trees planted and a consecration ceremony performed by C. J. Blomfield, the Bishop of London. Unfortunately it had also become clear that more capital would be needed to carry the business forward. Plans to build flanking subsidiary chapels for Roman Catholics and Non-Conformists were shelved – permanently as it turned out, though the Dissenters were eventually supplied with cramped accommodation in the northern gatehouse. A short-term loan to tide over immediate cash-flow problems was advanced by Robert Gunter. The number of burials remained, however – from a strictly commercial

146. The Arts and Crafts monument of Frederick Leyland (1831-1892), shipowner and noted patron of the Pre-Raphaelites. The tomb was designed by Sir Edwin Burne-Jones.

viewpoint – disappointing. In 1841 there were only 89, in 1842, 285. When cracks began to appear in the catacombs Baud tried to blame the contractor but he successfully argued that the architect had passed the work as fit and so it was Baud who was dismissed. Not until 1850 were the company's financial difficulties finally cleared up but it was still only achieving for its investors a deeply disappointing return of 1.5%. In 1851-2, in a hesitant and acrimonious series of negotiations, the newly-constituted Board of Health used its powers of compulsory purchase to acquire the cemetery for about half of what it had cost in outlays.

By 1889 some 155,000 interments had taken place. In that year a memorial was erected in honour of the Brigade of Guards. Another memorial, in the form of an obelisk, commemorates some 2,500 'Chelsea Pensioners'. These military memorials are collective and anonymous. But no less than 144 of the cemetery's permanent residents merit an individual entry in the *Dictionary of National Biography*. Although Brompton never attempted to group its more distinguished occupants in 'cluster burials' akin to Westminster Abbey's Poet's Corner it may be convenient to list some of them in categories. Many of the names are mentioned elsewhere in this book as residents. Not surprisingly, considering the distinctive character of Brompton as a residential area, there are many 'theatricals': Helena Faucit; 'Breezy' Bill Terriss; monocled Sir Squire Bancroft; impresario Sir Augustus Glossop Harris; Nellie Farren (1848-1904) burlesque idol of the Gaiety and grand-daughter of William Farren; Tom Foy, 'the Yorkshire Lad' (1866-1917); veteran actor-manager Benjamin Webster (1797-1882), an associate of both Mme. Vestris and Dion Boucicault; and *farceur* Brandon Thomas. Music numbers composer G.H.B. Rodwell; Blanche Roosevelt, the first American woman to sing Italian opera at Covent Garden; much-loved Austrian tenor Richard Tauber (1891-1948), whose grave is still covered with fresh flowers over half a century after his death; and the ashes of composer Constant Lambert (1905-51). Men of business are represented by the eponymous founders of a famed auction house and shipping line, Samuel Leigh Sotheby (1805-61) and Sir Samuel Cunard (1787-1865); by ship-owner and enthusiastic patron of the Pre-Raphaelites, Frederick Leyland (1831-92), whose elegant tomb was designed by Sir Edward Burne-Jones; by architects Thomas Cundy II (died 1895), George Godwin and Francis Fowke, Fowke's patron Sir Henry Cole and Godwin's employer Sir Charles Freake; and by Sir Henry Mears, another successful builder who in 1905 founded adjacent Chelsea Football Club. Technology is represented by railway engineers Sir John Fowler and C.B. Vignoles and Bennet Woodcroft, propeller expert and patent supremo. Outstanding medical practitioners include William Banting (1797-1878), whose surname originally became synonymous with slimming, and pioneer anaesthetist John Snow (1813-59), who also first demonstrated that cholera was a water-borne disease. The world of letters is represented by a diversity ranging from the self-dramatising George Borrow and W.H. Russell to the earnest Samuel Smiles (1812-1904), prophet of 'Self-Help' and the author of hundreds of 'ripping yarns' G.A. Henty (1832-1902). From the world of the arts

148. A relief on the tomb of Samuel Sotheby (1805-61), auctioneer and antiquarian, depicting the Expulsion from Eden.

147. The sumptuous sarcophagus of Val Prinsep (1838-1904), Pre-Raphaelite painter, dilettante and socialite.

149. Memorial to Dr John Snow (1813-58), pioneer of the use of ether and chloroform, who proved conclusively that cholera spread due to polluted water supplies.

151. The tomb of Dr Benjamin Golding (1793-1863), founder of Charing Cross Hospital.

there are the topographical water-colourist George Scharf, designer Godfrey Sykes and dilettante painter Val Prinsep (1838-1904), son-in-law of Frederick Leyland. Sportsmen include boxer 'Gentleman' John Jackson (1769-1845), champion of all England 1795-1803; Robert Coombes (1808-60) champion sculler of the Thames and the Tyne; and Percy Lambert (1881-1913), the first man to drive at 100 m.p.h., who was killed taking one last crack at breaking his own record. Public affairs are represented by reformer Sir James Kay-Shuttleworth and the doyenne of the suffragette movement, Emmeline Pankhurst (1858-1928). The number of generals interred in Brompton is legion, many knighted. There are several holders of the Victoria Cross. But no hero has a more graphic memorial than Flight Sub- Lieutenant Warneford (1891-1915) who was killed bringing down a Zeppelin over Ghent. Readers of the *Daily Express* subscribed for his memorial.

150. The suitably embellished monument to Augustus Harris (1852-96), impresario and manager of both Theatre Royal Drury Lane and Covent Garden Theatre.

Leisure

Earl's Court Exhibition was built on land bought by the Metropolitan District Railway Company in the 1860s and then found to be surplus to its requirements. In the 1870s the site seemed destined to accommodate 'Kensington Catholic Public School', ambitiously projected by Monsignor T. J. Capel as a feeder for an embryonic Catholic University College. The scheme collapsed in 1878 following Capel's disgrace over financial irregularities and alleged homosexual associations. Subsequent proposals to develop the area for housing foundered on difficulties of access and the noise from passing trains.

The idea of using the location for exhibitions came from John Robinson Whitley (1843-1922), manager of a Leeds engineering firm who had had experience of industrial exhibiting in Europe. While travelling in the US in 1884 Whitley met a consortium of businessmen eager to stage an 'American Exhibition' in London. Whitley forged a working partnership between that group and the District Railway, whose directors were keenly aware that the proposed exhibition site was within walking distance of four stations – Earl's Court, West Brompton, West Kensington and Addison Road (now Kensington Olympia). Visiting Washington in 1886 to enlist President Cleveland's support, Whitley chanced to witness the arrival there of the 'Buffalo Bill Roughriders and Redskin Show' and promptly booked it to be the star attraction of his opening season.

The complex that Whitley created consisted of three components. The first, accessible from Warwick Road, was an arena and covered stand, designed to Colonel Cody's verbal instructions and built by Peto Brothers. The second, squeezed between tracks and sidings and entered from Richmond Road, was a long, narrow single-storey exhibition building with annexes for refreshments. The third element was a pleasure garden including such attractions as a switchback railway, toboggan slide and London's largest bandstand. The three sites were linked by seven bridges over various railway lines and, in the delicately judged phrase of the *Survey of London*, "landscaped to give a superficial air of rural isolation". Only the arena and stand were actually in Kensington, the other two parts lying just over its western boundary, in Fulham.

Two, one thousand-strong gangs alternated day and night shifts to complete construction in four months. Work was still unfinished on opening day – 9 May 1887 – and what had been completed looked distinctly slight and sparse.

152. *The water splash or water toboggan at Earl's Court.*

153. *Programme for the Buffalo Bill show at Earl's Court.*

Critics thought the entrance fee too high. But Buffalo Bill confounded all prophets of gloom. Cowboys, Indians, Mexicans, the saga of the Pony Express, a pioneer wagon train, a girl sharp-shooter, bucking broncoes and a thrilling buffalo hunt combined to launch entranced Britons on a lifelong love-affair with the drama and romance of the 'Wild West'. The show was a smash hit, attracting an average daily gate of fifteen thousand people over a five month season and grossing over £350,000, or, as Col. Cody put it, "a barrel of money". Gladstone went. The Prince of Wales went too and, accompanied by the kings of Denmark, Greece, Belgium and Saxony, was driven round the arena in the Deadwood stage, surrounded by war-whooping warriors. The Queen went and patted the cheeks of selected papooses. Harrow School went – all of it. When the show finally closed at the end of October *The Times* pronounced its final verdict – " The Wild West was irresistible".

Earl's Court's American theme was followed in successive years by Italian, French, Spanish and German seasons but none could repeat the initial success of the Wild West show. In 1892 horticulture was tried, in 1893 forestry, plus the added attraction of a lake, made by flooding the arena, and Britain's first 'water-toboggan'. A new era opened with the advent of the Hungarian entrepreneur Imre Kiralfy (d. 1919), who had learned the trade of showman with Barnum and Bailey in the USA and envisaged giving the site a complete make-over. The 1894 season was essentially a 'filler', occupied by an industrial exhibition, while a new lease was negotiated, capital raised and work begun on constructing a three hundred foot-high 'Great Wheel'. It did not meet with universal approval. The fashionable writer Ouida observed acidly that " The fact that the great wheel of Earl's Court should attract sane persons as a diversion will alone prove how completely the instinct of correct taste, with its accompanying abhorrence of deformity, has become extinct in all modern crowds."

The wheel was inaugurated, along with a 5000-seater Empire Theatre and Queen's Court exhibition building, overlooking an artificial lake, mid-way through the 1895 season, which was devoted to 'The Empire of India'. The Wheel survived until 1907, when it ceased to be profitable and was disassembled, having carried some 2,500,000 passengers over the course of its lifetime. The 1895 India theme was carried over into 1896. In 1898 came 'Our Naval Victories', in 1901 a re-enactment of the Boxer Rising – 'China, or the Relief of the Legations' and in 1902 the coronation of Edward VII provided a ready-made focus.

154. The Great Wheel at Earl's Court c.1900. Philbeach Gardens is behind the wheel.

Robert Machray's 1902 book *The Night Side of London* devotes a whole chapter to Earl's Court, which he characterised as the lineal descendant of Vauxhall and Cremorne, the premier pleasure-gardens of the Georgian and early Victorian periods respectively. Machray's endorsement was enthusiastic:

> " The vast extent of Earl's Court, the diversity of the attractions of all kinds it furnishes, the picturesqueness of its grounds, its myriads of coloured lights, its magnificent music ... have given it a unique place in the life of the town. Of a summer's evening there is no more agreeable lounge to be found anywhere, nor is there anything like it in any other city in the world. It seems strange that there is not something of the sort in Paris, but there is not."

Much credit was given to Kiralfy personally: "The Director-General of Earl's Court (a native of Buda-Pest) is a man who has a veritable Oriental love of gorgeous display and sensuous

155. A District Railway ad in 1897 extolling the virtues of the Victorian Era Exhibition. Combined rail and entrance tickets were available.

magnificence. He has a positive genius for contriving a great spectacle. To his native fondness for it he adds a wide experience gained in the United States ...".

Alas, the *genius locii* was about to depart and with Kiralfy went his élan and imaginative flair. From 1906 onwards Kiralfy withdrew from Earl's Court to concentrate on building the White City complex for the projected 1908 London Olympiad. The decision to make Hungary the theme of Earl's Court's 1908 season may be interpreted either as a legacy or a tribute. Earl's Court continued in business but the management lacked Kiralfy's vision. In 1910 the premises passed from London Exhibitions Ltd. to Earl's Court Ltd. but this represented no breakthrough.

When the Great War broke out in the autumn of 1914 a million Belgian refugees fled their homeland. Of these, a hundred thousand took ship direct to Britain and Earl's Court served as the largest single centre for their initial reception, accommodation and processing. After the war it reverted to railway ownership, part serving as a bus depot, other areas staging occasional

156. Traditional leisure venues were local pubs, a number of which dated to the 17th century. Pictured here is the Swan Tavern, Brompton in 1871. Sketch by J.T. Wilson.

157. The White Hart, Earl's Court in 1867. Drawing by J.T. Wilson.

158. The Ship tavern, where Queen's Gate now meets Old Brompton Road, c.1830.

159. The Old George, Cranley Terrace (today's 50-74 Fulham Road) by T. H. Shepherd c.1850. It was replaced by the Cranley Arms.

circuses or falling into decay. The Theatre, now known as the Empress Hall, was used for storage and as a workshop. Plans were mooted for the theatre's conversion to an ice-hockey rink but failed to materialise. Renewal finally came in 1935 when the London Passenger Transport Board promised a new 99-year lease to a reconstituted Earl's Court Ltd with significant American backers. In 1936-7 the present building of reinforced concrete was erected to the designs of Chicago architect C. Howard Crane at a cost of £1,500,000. Its main facade strongly resembled an unbuilt design for an 'International Music Hall and Opera House', intended for Hyde Park Corner and designed by an architectural consortium of which Crane was a member. Inside it offered 450,000 square feet of exhibition space unimpeded by columns. Nowadays Earl's Court hosts some 130 events and 70 conferences annually, receiving over 3,000,000 visitors.

HOTELS

Bailey's Hotel was purpose built in 1875-6 on a reserved site immediately overlooking Gloucester Road station. James Bailey (1840-1910), a Norfolk man, lived on the premises with his family and a live-in staff of thirty-five. Bailey's stated objective was that the enterprise should "in all respects be conducted in the most respectable manner". It appears to have been an immediate success, as the premises were extended in 1877, again in 1881 and again in 1883, to add bedrooms, put a bow window on the ballroom, create a mansarded attic and establish a garden, at the expense of knocking down a block of stables but recently erected. The public areas featured marbled columns and stained-glass windows. In 1890 electricity was installed along with an 'American elevator'. Americans, who generally held no high opinion of English hotels, constituted an important target market and it seems that Bailey's hit it. A contemporary guidebook assured transatlantic travellers that they would find themselves in "rich and substantial surroundings" with the most up to date sanitation, stringent fire precautions and an excellent wine cellar but also with a "cosey, homelike atmosphere" and all in "the healthiest and most fashionable part of London". Bailey sold up in 1894, became an MP the following year and sat on the boards of Harrods and D.H. Evans. Residing at 58 Rutland Gate, he also had a £60,000 estate in Essex. He was knighted in 1905 and quit the Commons in 1906.

Bailey's eventually had some three hundred apartments. Its success made it the nucleus for other imitators, but far smaller and accommo-

160. Bailey's Hotel by Gloucester Road station.

dated in converted houses, rather than purpose-built premises. By 1914 fourteen such establishments occupied eighteen former houses in the Cromwell Road and Harrington Gardens. In the inter-war period they expanded into a further seven houses, many of their clients being long-term residents, rather than tourists. Two decades of relative stagnation followed until the building of the West London Air Terminal (1957) on Cromwell Road and the tourism boom of the 1960s revitalised existing establishments and, aided by the 1969 Development of Tourism Act, which provided a public subsidy of £1,000 per bedroom, stimulated the construction of the monster blocks which now tower over the main artery leading out to Heathrow – the London (now Swallow) International (1968-72), Forum (originally London Penta) (1971-2), Elizabetta (1972) and Gloucester (1972-3). Pevsner, normally a fan of modern movement buildings, was unimpressed, dismissing the Forum as "unnecessarily aggressive" and the Swallow as "one of the more unforgivable additions to the borough."

161. An Earl's Court attraction in 1937 was James's Turkish Baths in Earl's Court Gardens.

162. *Women cyclists at the Wheel Club at Hereford House, Bolton Gardens in 1896.*

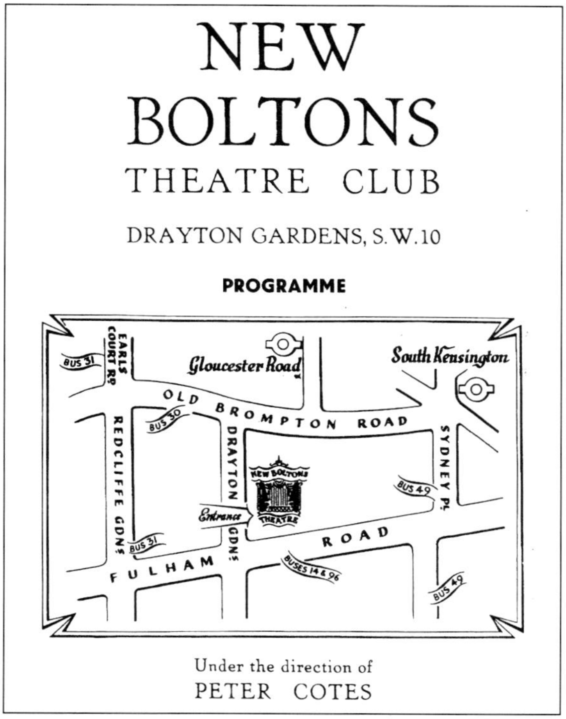

163. *Advertisement for an amateur dramatic club in Drayton Gardens c.1950s*

164. *The West London Air Terminal in Cromwell Road. Despite the long haul from the nearest Underground station encumbered with suitcases, it was the most convenient way to get to Heathrow before the Underground line was built there.*

Shopping

Maria Perry's witty *divertissement Knightsbridge Woman* boldly asserts that "Shopping is the universal pursuit of the Knightsbridge classes." Brompton, invariably in the context of shopping, styled Knightsbridge, has some two centuries of retailing heritage behind it. Harvey Nichols, a favourite of international glitterati such as Joan Collins, Jamie Lee Curtis and the late Princess of Wales, was founded in 1813 by Benjamin Harvey as an emporium for the sale of linens and silks at what was then known as Lowndes Terrace. It later branched out into Oriental carpets and benefited greatly from the success of the Great Exhibition of 1851. Mr Harvey bequeathed the business to his daughter, Elizabeth, who took a heavy hint that she should take their silk buyer, Colonel Nichols, into partnership. The ancestral founders of The Scotch House, the Gardiner brothers of Glasgow, arrived with their tartans and tweeds in 1830 to cash in on the fashion craze promoted by George IV, and, less consciously, by the hugely popular novels of Sir Walter Scott. Harrod's, dates from the succeeding generation.

The changing character of Brompton Road as a shopping centre is clearly chronicled in street directories. Cardinal Newman complained sniffily that the site selected for the future Brompton Oratory in 1853 was in "a neighbourhood of second-rate gentry and second-rate shops". A street directory near-contemporary (1859) to this observation indeed reveals a positively homely selection of retail establishments, then catering primarily for local, daily needs. The two dozen businesses comprising the section then known as Middle Queen's Buildings, where Harrod's now stands, were primarily concerned with food and dress. A grocer (Harrod's), greengrocer, butcher, pork butcher and dairyman existed alongside a baker, a muffin baker and a 'confectioner and haircutter'. There were three tailors, a straw hat maker and a bootmaker. Other trades included leatherseller, 'glass bottle dealer', bookbinder, linendraper and a carpenter and undertaker. In the same year the alleyways around Montpelier Square still housed at least two 'cowkeepers'. T. Crofton Croker's *A Walk from London to Fulham*, published in book form in 1860, treats Brompton Road as still an essentially residential, rather than commercial, thoroughfare.

KNIGHTSBRIDGE.—We advise Sheard, tea grocer, to give better weight.

We advise the butter slappers at Dixon's, Queen. Building's, not to come it quite so strong with the servant girls.

We advise the monkeyfied counter jumpers, at Harvey's, Corner of Sloane-st., not to fancy all the girls in love with them.

We advise Mrs. Powter, at the coffee shop, Sloane-st. to be more civil to her customers·

We advise Miss Betsey Wright, sister to the above, at the same coffee shop, net to make such a fool of herself with the cabmen, and to alter her temper or she will never get a husband.

We advise Willisford, surgeon of Sloane-st., not to turn common informer.

We advise Jemmy Slyaut, alias, long Jemmy, of Lower Sloane-st., not to fancy all the girls in love with him, and not look down the areas, or he will have the Crusher after him.

We advise Joe Dickson, companion to the above, the same.

We advise Wm. Proper John, the spicy butcher, not to pay so much attention to the pretty Mary Nelson, but to attend to selling the block ornaments.

We advise Charley Proper John, not to gormandize so much.

We adviae Miss Ann Moss, not to drink so much gin, and not get so lushey on Saturday nights.

We advise Mrs Taylor, not to care for being shown up in the Paul Pry.

We advise Moore, the barber, on the Green, not to cut such a swagger rattling his money.

We advise Charles, the salesman, of Middle Row, not to come it so strong with the girls at the cutler's next door.

We advise Hill, the chandler-shop keeper, not to laugh at other people in the Paul Pry.

We advire Mrs. Dale, and her daughters, not to talk about their neighbours.

We advise James Fraser, Publican, Rose & Crown, not to drink whiskey at other peoples expence.

wife. There is no harm in her going to Mr. Cox's, with her half-pint pot, so many times a day, provided she did not make herself so little thought of, by sitting in the tap-room with a parcel of men.

165. A Paul Pry scandal sheet of c.1850 naming and shaming Brompton and Knightsbridge traders and residents.

A generation later (1894) the sustained rise in middle-class incomes and local population which characterised the second half of the nineteenth century is reflected in the full-scale commercialisation of both sides of the Brompton Road from end to end. Alongside surviving purveyors of items of daily consumption were ranged a far more comprehensive and diverse selection of specialist suppliers. One cluster was clearly related to the nearby presence of Tattersall's (*see p136*) and consisted, side by side, of a coachbuilders, harness maker, whip manufacturer and a saddler, as well as the head office of the Hunt Servants' Benefit Society. What one might call decor consumption was represented by self-differentiated businesses distinguishing themselves as a 'curiosity dealer', fine art dealer, dealer in

166. Part of an advertisement for Louise & Co, bonnet makers of 59 Brompton Road in 1895, who also had a large shop in Shoreditch High Street.

167. Harrod's shop in 1892, before its palatial rebuilding.

antiquities (2), and antique furniture dealer (4) plus six booksellers and an 'importer of birds'. Many premises still involved manufacture on the spot as well as selling direct to customers. Examples included makers of watches, cycles, umbrellas, ladders, stays, fans, blinds, portmanteaux and elastic bandages. Service industries were represented by numerous doctors and dressmakers, a phrenologist, teachers of fencing and the mandolin, three 'photographic artists', the Sanitary Woollen Cleaning Company and the South Kensington School of Massage and Electricity.

Twenty years later, on the eve of the Great War, the retailing revolution had rolled on to give Brompton Road a distinctively different appearance once again. One specially noticeable development was the incursion of what have subsequently become household 'High Street' names – Ryman the stationers, Findlater's the wine merchant, Dollond the opticians, Freeman, Hardy and Willis' shoe shop and three branches of J. Lyons and Co. New technologies were represented by a retail branch of Kodak and showrooms or dealerships for Humber and Peugeot and no less than six other agents for motor cars. As the private car was very definitely a luxury product this concentration of the motor trade bespeaks a very high level of local affluence, confirmed by the simultaneous presence of eight 'court dressmakers' and three 'court milliners'. The enhancement of femininity was further provided for by 'Madame Georgette, electrolysis operator', with a manicurist virtually next door and two masseuses a few further steps away. Other distinctive businesses, unlikely to have been readily found in other parts of the metropolis, included 'Yoshimoto and Co., Japanese fancy goods importers', a vegetarian restaurant and an American dentist.

HARROD'S

Harrod's has become sufficiently a national institution to rate its own entry in Bamber Gascoigne's *Encyclopaedia of Britain,* where it is characterised as "Britain's most famous department store". The *Guinness Guide to Superlative London* goes one better to call it "the world's most famous department store" and emphasises that it is "comparable to a small town and ... every bit as self-sufficient", with its own power

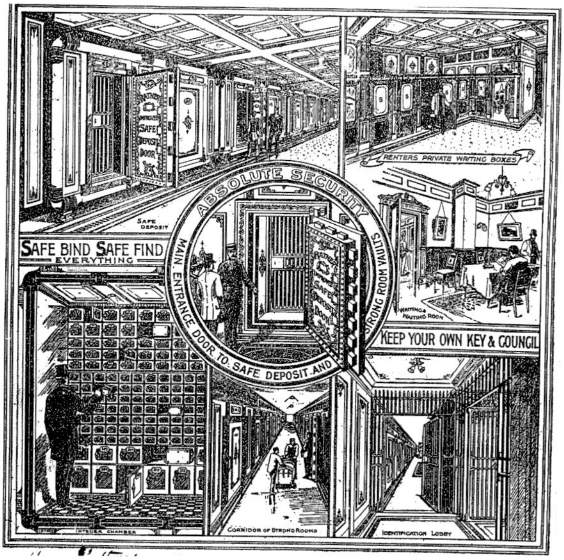

168. An advertisement for Harrod's security vault in 1893.

station and even three wells. The store which once boasted the telegraphic address 'Everything, London', began modestly when, between 1849 and 1853, Henry Charles Harrod (1800-85), an Essex miller who had become a tea merchant from Eastcheap in the City, took over the grocery business of a troubled client, Philip Burden. Its address was then known as 8 Middle Queen's Buildings and it traded in a converted house dating from *c.* 1781-3. Nothing much changed until the proprietorship passed to Henry's twenty-year-old son, Charles Digby Harrod, who bought out his father in stages between 1861 and 1864. For the first twenty years Harrod operated on a strict 'cash only' basis, which did not seem to inhibit a steady expansion. (Customers were offered a free delivery service.) By 1867 he was employing five assistants and by 1868 had a turnover of £1,000 a week. Diversifying into non-perishables such as stationery, perfumes and patent medicines, by 1870 he was employing sixteen assistants, at a total wage-bill of £15 a week. In 1873 a two-storey extension to the premises was built over the back garden and by 1880 the staff roll-call had expanded dramatically to reach a hundred and the business marked a new maturity by offering its customers a range of 'own label' groceries. Disaster in the shape of a hugely destructive fire struck in 1883. For many businesses the setback might have proved terminal but Harrod turned it to brilliant advantage by a stroke of marketing genius, writing to all customers to assure them that, although outstanding orders might be delayed briefly, they would be fulfilled. This bravura display of 'customer care' enabled the store to double its business by the following year. Reversing his previous policy, in 1885 Harrod introduced credit accounts for approved customers who included Ellen Terry, Oscar Wilde and royal mistress Lillie Langtry.

In 1889 Harrod's became a limited company. Charles Digby Harrod took a large cash sum and retired to become the first occupant of 31 Evelyn Gardens. The business went into a precipitate decline. A saviour was swiftly found in the person of Richard Burbidge (1847-1917) who had already worked miracles at Harrod's main rivals, Whiteley's. Burbidge, a restless workaholic, achieved a virtual re-launch of the business. Over the course of twenty years its two hundred staff became six thousand and its profits expanded ten-fold. In 1913 Harrod's received the accolade of a Royal Warrant from Queen Mary and Burbidge was knighted shortly afterwards. The Burbidge dynasty remained in charge of top management until Harrod's became part of the House of Fraser group in the 1950s. Following its take-over by Mr Al-Fayed it reverted to the status of a private company in 1986.

The present Harrod's store, extending over an entire block, was rebuilt piecemeal between 1894 and 1912, as part of Burbidge's relaunch, taking in the site of other previously existing businesses, the Friend at Hand public house and an elementary school. Designed by C.W. Stephens, the architect of Claridges hotel, to which it bears a distinct stylistic resemblance, it was praised for its exuberance and scale "if not for architectural finesse". The reincarnated Harrod's featured London's first 'moving staircase', a proto-escalator installed in 1898, and the spectacular ceramic murals in the Food Hall, conceived by W.J. Neatby and executed by Doulton in 1903. By then Harrod's had become the world's largest department store, as well as arguably the most famous, justifying the slogan enshrined on its terra-cotta facade *Omnia Omnibus Ubique* – Everything for Everybody Everywhere. In the year that Harrod's remodelling was substantially completed the store employed a model whose son grew up to become the travel writer Eric Newby. In his autobiography *A Traveller's Life* Newby pays his mother's old employer the unique compliment of an entire chapter.

169. *(Above) The courtyard of the old Tattersall's building near Hyde Park Corner.*

170. *The new Tattersall building at Knightsbridge Green, opposite Sloane Street.*

TATTERSALL'S

Tattersall's, for over a century synonymous with horse-flesh, is now commemorated only by the name of a public house. Richard Tattersall was a former stud groom to the second Duke of Kingston who had a fine house at No. 3 Knightsbridge and was described by the waspish Horace Walpole as "a very weak man, of the greatest beauty and finest person in England ". Richard Tattersall was also a well-set-up fellow himself but, more to the point, a man of shining integrity. Following his employer's death, he set himself up as an auctioneer in 1766 and soon afterwards established premises near Hyde Park Corner with stables, loose boxes and an enclosure for trying out horses. There were also subscription rooms for members of the Jockey Club, which became not only the social centre for members of the racing fraternity but also the *de facto* regulatory centre for betting on the turf. Tattersall's had already become sufficient of an institution by 1782 to be mentioned in a stage-play. When Tattersall's original 99-year lease expired in 1865 the premises were demolished to make way for an extension to St George's Hospital and the business moved to two acres

of stabling at Knightsbridge Green. In 1909 London historian E. Beresford Chancellor could still write that "one could no more imagine the town without it than one could conceive it without St Paul's or Charing Cross station." Alas, the unimaginable eventually happened and in 1939 Tattersall's moved out to Newmarket.

BEAUCHAMP PLACE

In 1972 the London Tourist Board selected Beauchamp Place as the best single shopping street in the entire metropolis. Considering that it began as a side-street of speculator's cottages in the 1820s its rise to such eminence is, indeed, remarkable; but it was not quite so sudden as has sometimes been suggested. The commercialisation of Beauchamp Place and in particular its connections with high fashion and antiques pre-date the First World War. In 1914 only five of its sixty-odd premises were still in private residential use, plus one more sub-divided into apartments. No less than a dozen court dressmakers were established there, plus half a dozen court milliners and individual makers of corsets, false teeth and wigs. Six antique dealers were also present, their premises interspersed with

172. A bespoke bootmaker's in Beauchamp Place, 1903.

171. Beauchamp Place, c.1905.

173. *The premises of J.J. Allen, house furnishers, at 130 Brompton Road, c.1905.*

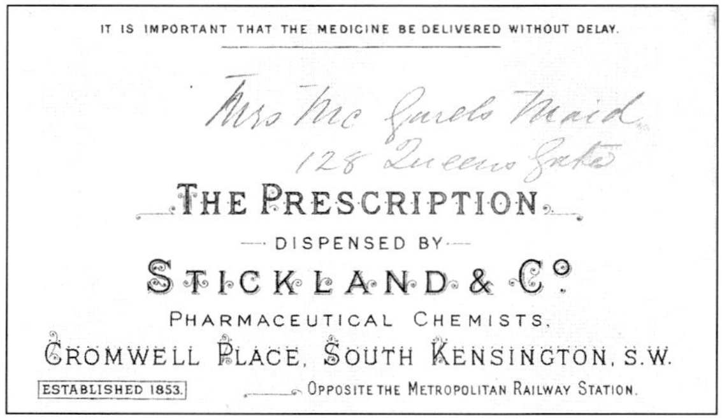

174. *A prescription envelope issued by chemists Stickland & Co of Cromwell Place, for the treatment of a maid at 128 Queen's Gate.*

the more prosaic services offered by a sweep, a plumber and a vet.

A generation later, in 1950, the 'court' distinction had become passé but the number of dressmakers and milliners had increased to thirty and been joined by four furriers. The antique dealers, now eight in number, had been joined by five retailers of modern furnishings and interior design services. The wig-maker had been replaced by three hairdressers and the maker of false teeth by five beauticians, backed by two chiropodists and two physiotherapists.

Other Beauchamp Place businesses included four photographers, four tourist bureaux, four agencies supplying domestic staff or cleaning services, a specialist supplier of potted shrimps and 'Dogs' Baths and Requisites Ltd.'

In 1993 the *Virgin Insiders' Guide to London* was to observe snootily: "Beauchamp Place was one of London's coolest streets in the late seventies and early eighties, but it has failed to keep its reputation from being tarnished by the arrival of very cheap discount shops and places selling expensive rubbish." It is not clear in which category the *Guide* would have placed Bruce Oldfield, Caroline Charles, Isabell Kristensen or Janet Reger, although it did have some half kind words for Margaret Howell: "should be Britain's answer to Armani ... If you want to start looking a bit more serious about how you dress, this is not a bad place to start." Other denizens of Beauchamp Place include the Duke of Edinburgh's shirtmakers, Ashley and Blake and Dame Diana Rigg's tailor, Edward Sexton. Maria Perry (1995) remains an unrepentant fan: " Beauchamp Place is the Mecca of shoppers who are *real* Ladies ... *Real* ladies own some of the shops, too. Lady Tryon sells frocks ... under the sign of Kanga, a nickname given her by the Prince of Wales ...' Annabel Jones 'is really the maiden name of Lady Astor ... Caroline Charles and Janet Reger are not *real* Ladies, but they are real people."

BOUTIQUE BOROUGH?

At the very time that the London Tourist Board was awarding Beauchamp Place its accolade as shopping street of the metropolis, concerned local residents were voicing worries that tourism was turning their neighbourhood into a "boutique borough" in which small shops had been "engulfed in a tidal wave of gourmet restaurants, chic boutiques and exclusive delicatessens." A survey calculated that, while food shopping in the locality had contracted by a third between 1966 and 1971, the presence of restaurants, hairdressers, dry cleaners and similar service providers had expanded by half. The passage of time may have slowed that rate of change but has done little to reverse its direction.

Chronology

1628 Smith's Charity established
1636 Swan tavern first mentioned
1681 Brompton Park Nursery founded
1700 Robert Furber establishes a nursery at Kensington Gore
1726 Turnpike trust established for Brompton Road
1748 Hull's Academy relocates to Earl's Court
1749 Site of Holy Trinity used as St. George's Hospital burial ground
1757 'The Terrace' built at Earl's Court by carpenter Roger Blagrave
1770 ca. Brompton Villa built
1774 ca. The Rosary built
1777 Swan tavern rebuilt
1784 Balloon ascent from Lochee's military academy
1785 Michael Novosielski begins development of Egerton Place
1789 William Curtis establishes subscription Botanic Gardens at Brompton
1790 Florida Gardens bankrupt
1813 Harvey Nichols founded
1815 Hereford House built
1818 Trevor Square built
1819 Blemell House school opened
1821 Brompton Square begun
1828 Kensington Canal opened
George Basevi appointed Surveyor to Smith's Charity estate
Western Grammar School founded
1829 Holy Trinity, Brompton
1832 Bankruptcy of Harrison's nursery
1833 Pelham Place and Crescent built
Edwardes' Kensington estate entailed
1836 Kensington Canal sold to Birmingham and Great Western Railway
1840 Thurloe Square begun
Brompton cemetery consecrated
1842 Brompton National School opened
1843 Egerton Crescent and Terrace built
1844-56 The Billings area built
1845 Bunch of Grapes public house, Brompton Road built
Onslow Square and Hereford Square begun
1846 Bute House demolished
1849-53 Henry Charles Harrod acquires Burden's grocery
1850 Cowper House demolished
St Mary, Boltons consecrated
1851-60 The Boltons built
1851 The Great Exhibition
Soyer's Gastronomic Symposium
Gloucester Lodge demolished
1851-2 Board of Health takes over Brompton Cemetery
1853 Hale House demolished
1855 Cromwell Road laid out
1857 Gore House demolished
'Brompton Boilers' opened
1859 Kensington Canal filled in
1860 St Paul's, Onslow Square consecrated
1861 Royal Horticultural Society gardens opened
Death of Albert, Prince Consort
1862 International Exhibition held on Cromwell Road site
1865 Onslow Gardens begun
Hollywood Arms public house, Holywood Road begun
1867 Harrington Road laid out
1868 Prince of Teck public house built
1871 First Earl's Court station opened on the east side of the road
Albert Hall opened
1872 Brompton Boilers relocated to Bethnal Green Museum
1873-6 Hogarth Road built
1873-81 Longridge Road built
1875-6 Bailey's Hotel built
1875 Earl's Court station burns down
1876 Courtfield Hotel built
Albert Memorial completed
National Training School for Music opened
1878 Earl's Court station re-opens on present site
Bankruptcy of Corbett and McClymont, builders
1879 Earl's Court Farm demolished
Albert Hall Mansions built
1880-5 Nevern Square built
1880-94 Brompton Oratory built
1881 Natural History Museum opened
1883 International Fisheries Exhibition
1884 International Health Exhibition
City and Guilds Institute established at Earl's Court
1886 Earl's Court House demolished
1887 Buffalo Bill Wild West show at Earl's Court
St Cuthbert's, Philbeach Gardens conse crated
1888 Royal Horticultural Society gardens re moved from South Kensington site
1889 Harrod's becomes a limited company
1892 Savigear's riding school opened
1893 Imperial Institute opened
1894-1912 Harrod's rebuilt

1900 Hereford Lodge demolished
St Augustine's, Queen's Gate
1901-4 Coleherne Court built
1903 Holy Trinity, Prince Consort Road conse crated
1906 Brompton Road station opened
1906-7 Earl's Court Great Wheel demolished
1907 Closure of Earl's Court forge
Imperial College established
1909 Reconstructed Victoria & Albert museum opened
1911 Escalators installed at Earl's Court station
1912 Royal Geographical Society acquires Lowther Lodge
1913 Harrod's awarded a royal warrant
1914 Earl's Court Exhibition houses Belgian refugees
1921 Rawlplug Company established
Park House, Earl's Court Road demolished
1927 Hoop and Toy rebuilt
1928 Science Museum opened
1934 Brompton Road station closed
1936-7 Earl's Court Exhibition rebuilt
1939 Tattersall's relocates to Newmarket
1952-3 Brompton Chapel converted to Bonham's
1957 West London Air Terminal opens on Cromwell Road
Bousfield School relocates to The Boltons
1958 Imperial Institute reconstituted as Com monwealth Institute
1968-72 Swallow International hotel built
1971-2 Forum hotel built
1972 Beauchamp Place nominated best shopping street in London
1973 Earl's Court Conservation Area designated
Earl's Court YWCA rebuilt
1975 Earl's Court Square Conservation Area designated
St Peter's, Cranley Gardens reconsecrated as an Armenian cathedral
1986 Harrod's reverts to private company status

Further Reading

Giles Alington: *The Earl's Court Village* (1995)
Sean Callery: *Harrods, Knightsbridge : The Story of Society's Favourite Store* (1991)
E. Beresford Chancellor: *Knightsbridge and Belgravia* (1909)
Chapman, Taylor Partners: *Brompton: Conservation Area Proposals Statement* (Royal Borough of Kensington and Chelsea 1988)
Thomas Crofton Croker: *A Walk from London to Fulham* (1860, enlarged ed. 1896)
Denny, Barbara: *Kensington Past* (1998)
Dictionary of National Biography
Geoffrey Evans: *Kensington* (1975)
Rachel Ferguson: *Royal Borough* (1950)
Brian Girling: *Kensington : The Archive Photographs Series* (1996)
Edward Lee: *Musical London* (1995)
Robert Machray: *The Night Side of London* (1902)
Maria Perry: *Knightsbridge Woman* (1995)
Nikolaus Pevsner: *The Buildings of England: London 3 North-West* (1991)
Dorothy Stroud: *The Thurloe Estate* (1965)
Dorothy Stroud: *The South Kensington Estate of Henry Smith's Charity : Its History and Development* (1975)
William T. Stearn: *The Natural History Museum at South Kensington* (1981)
Survey of London Vol XXXVIII: The Museums Area of South Kensington and Westminster (1975)
Survey of London Vol XLI: South Kensington: Brompton (1983)
Survey of London Vol XLII: Southern Kensington – Kensington Square to Earl's Court (1986)
Annabel Walker: *Kensington and Chelsea: a social and architectural history* (1987)
Giles Walkley: *Artists' Houses in London 1764-1914* (1994)

E.J. Willson: *West London Nursery Gardens* (1982)

INDEX

Illustrations are indicated by asterisks